RUSSIA

MONGOLIA

CHINA

BURMA

LAOS

THAILAND

CAMBODIA

VIETNAM

JAPAN

PHILIPPINES

MALAYSIA

INDONESIA

TIGER!

This book accompanies the "In The Wild" television special about the tiger presented by Bob Hoskins. His long-held fascination with tigers led him to undertake a 20,000 mile journey exploring the physical and spiritual world of the tiger.

Bob Hoskins and his camera team traveled to India, Nepal and Indonesia. Three of the Indonesian islands - Java, Bali and Sumatra - once had tigers. Now there are only a handful in Sumatra. India and Nepal are generally considered to be the heartland of the tiger's range, yet tiger numbers have halved in just a few years. If nothing is done to remedy this situation, the tiger faces extinction.

The tiger is a creature the world cannot afford to lose. In the following pages Simon Barnes investigates this extraordinary animal, explains why it is in danger of becoming extinct, and what we need to do to save it.

TIGER!

SIMON BARNES

Foreword by

BOB HOSKINS

Scientific Consultant: PETER JACKSON

A·THOMAS·DUNNE BOOK

St. Martin's Press
New York

ACKNOWLEDGMENTS

Thanks to Ross Couper-Johnston, and Lucy Farmer. Further thanks to Baron
Robert Stjernstedt and Chris Brian who first introduced me to the genus
Panthera. Thanks to CLW and greetings to JDPB, hoping that there will be
some *Panthera* left for him.

Designed by Bill Mason
Color origination by Pica Color Separation, Singapore
Printed and bound in Portugal by Printer Portugesa
Library of Congress Cataloging-in-Publication Data is available on request.

ISBN: 0-312-11544-X

"A Thomas Dunne Book"

CONTENTS

FOREWORD

Opposite:

BOB HOSKINS, DURING FILMING OF TIGRESS PRODUCTIONS' SPECIAL "IN THE WILD", WITH A TIGER CUB. THE FILM EXPLORES HOSKINS' FASCINATION WITH THE TIGER.

Prior to spending a few nights on my own in a tent listening to the jungle, I always believed William Blake's enigmatic poem was just the result of too much opium. Being in the tiger's natural environment compelled me to picture mankind's earliest experiences, the memories we have inherited, when men hunted in packs and brought down the mammoth with only flint-tipped spears. Of families huddled together around spark-spitting fires, cave walls flickering with ever-changing stripes of black shadow and orange and white flame, a constant reminder of the sabertooth somewhere outside.

From the beginning, when men and tiger shared the hunting grounds, the 'Master Hunter' was always regarded with God-like respect. A wise pedagogue with powers beyond the physical. The living spirit of the ancient ancestors. The bringer of both life and death. The healer.

Tiger tracking early in the morning, on the back of Chan Chun Kali, my elephant. Softly trudging through the white mist that clings to the jungle floor, before the sun burns it off. Listening to the animal calls signalling the tiger's presence. Following the traces left only minutes before. The remains of a kill. The huge paw prints dotted along the soft river bank, that abruptly stop for no visible reason. The feeling of being watched. Knowing, although you can't see the tiger, the tiger can see you. It all became very clear. There, in the jungle where it belongs, the tiger is far more than just a big, dangerous, orange cat.

Somewhere between Rudyard Kipling's voracious man-eater and Winnie the Pooh's enthusiastic friend, lurks a primal mystery buried deep in the dreams and fears of us all. Think of lions and immediately strength and nobility spring to mind. Think of tigers and there are no words, just feelings.

Bob Hoskins

Right

The tiger's armor consists of more than teeth and claws: it is actually its mind that matters most. The tiger relies on skill, experience and knowledge for survival.

T O O T H

and

C L A W

FEARFUL SYMMETRY

MAMMALS DO NOT GET MORE FEARFUL THAN THE TIGER. THE CHAMPION OF ALL CATS: THE CHAMPION OF ALL CARNIVORES. PERHAPS THE MOST HANDSOME BEAST IN CREATION: CERTAINLY THE MOST EFFECTIVE AMBUSH PREDATOR ON THE PLANET. A SIZE BIGGER THAN THE LION AND ADAPTED TO WORK ALONE: EVERY GROWN-UP TIGER MUST KILL FOR ITSELF EVERY TIME IT WISHES TO EAT. SELF-RELIANT: INDEPENDENT: MASSIVE: THE TIGER IS ARGUABLY THE MOST SPECTACULAR KILLING MACHINE THAT NATURE HAS COME UP WITH, AT LEAST, IF WE DISCOUNT A CERTAIN MISCHIEVOUS APE.

The tiger kills animals as big as itself and bigger. Even the calves of the elephant and rhinoceros are within its range. Massive animals like gaur, a species of wild cattle, and sambar, a colossal deer, are taken regularly. The tiger must live without the endurance of dogs and wolves and without their advantage of hunting in packs. It must live without the speed of the cheetah, and without the cooperative life, the strategies, and the ferocious teamwork of the lion. The tiger is the big cat that walks by itself.

This is not to typecast the tiger as a bloodthirsty maniac: only one mammal deserves that description. The tiger kills to live but, for that matter, so does the robin in your back garden. The difference between killing worms and killing buffaloes is one of scale, not of principle. The tiger kills for food, and is sublimely effective. If we look for blind ferocity, frivolous killing, or for entire industries based on slaughter, we must look not to the tiger but to humankind. The tiger, like every killing species save one, is an innocent, and a beautiful innocent at that.

A tiger is no good in the chase. Once it gets involved in a race, it has already finished second. Nor is head-on confrontation a profitable technique. A tiger's job is to eat, not to pick fights. Like every other animal, it plays to its strengths. And one of its great strengths is, indeed, its strength. It kills in bursts of explosive power. A tiger hunt involves long, long hours of preparation and a few seconds of mayhem.

A tiger is the world's supreme silent killer: male and female alike are required by necessity, by their solitary lives, to hunt and to kill. A tiger's, or for that matter a tigress's, secondary weapons are its power, its speed over very short distances, claws for gripping and teeth for despatching the victim, eyes adapted for excellent night vision, good sense of smell, and a quite startlingly acute sense of hearing. But its number one weapon lies inside that broad, well-armed skull. Experience. Individual skill. Knowledge. Knowledge acquired by its own successes and failings: knowledge acquired from two years and more of the instruction and example of its mother: knowledge gained from watching sibling tigers: knowledge gained from scrapping and hunting games with its siblings in cubhood: knowledge gained from an ever growing understanding of its own patch of country and of the beasts that live there.

A tiger is the most jungle-smart predator of them all. It has to be. If a tiger cannot marry an almost impossible subtlety of approach to the frank mayhem of his charge, he will not eat. The comparison between a prowling jungle-smart tiger, and a prowling human who only thinks he is jungle-smart, is instructive. A distance of 50 yards (50m) that a man will cover in two minutes, believing he makes himself amazingly invisible and silent by taking such a time, will take a tiger 15 minutes. There have even been claims that rather than risk the faint crackle of a dead leaf, a tiger will instead slowly and silently crush the leaf into dust beneath his padded paw. If there is a whiff of the tall story about this claim, it shows something of the respect, the awe

Left

THE TIGER IS JUNGLE-
SMART. HUNTING
SUCCESS DEPENDS ON
THE DEPTH AND
EXTENT OF HIS
UNDERSTANDING OF
HIS TERRITORY AND OF
THE ANIMALS ON
WHICH HE PREYS.

Right:

HOMING IN ON THE
TARGET: A TIGER PRE-
PARES AN APPROACH
ON AN ISOLATED
CHINKARA, A SPECIES
OF GAZELLE.

Opposite:

DEATH GRIP. A TIGER
FROM THE
RANTHAMBHORE
RESERVE IN INDIA
ESTABLISHES THE
THROTTLE-GRIP ON A
CHITAL, ALSO KNOWN
AS A SPOTTED DEER.
THERE IS NO ESCAPE.

in which tigers are held by jungle-smart humans.

Killing is a far more straightforward matter. The technique of the tiger is all about getting close, and when a tiger does manage to get close, it is more or less all over bar the eating. It is the getting close that takes all a tiger's intelligence and skill. Once there, the tiger is simple, unsubtle and utterly devastating: a frantic rush of a few explosive bounds, and it is onto the selected beast. It is not a roaring, snarling performance of aggression: noisy behavior does not make sense for an ambushing hunter. The tiger can be noisy all right, but noise is normally reserved for fellow tigers. A successful hunting tiger is silent and decisive. A tiger will normally attack from the side, or from behind, or at some angle between the two. Most large prey must be knocked down in the pell-mell charge. This is not normally a melodramatic flying leap: the tiger usually stays in contact with the ground. But these are not beasts that live by strict routines: bigger animals sometimes provoke more spectacular assaults. Tigers have even been seen riding on the backs of big animals such as sambar or domestic buffalo for brief periods, but the aim of virtually every attack is to get underneath.

With his spring, the tiger may well get a hold onto the victim with his teeth, aiming at the shoulder or the the neck, but from there, once he has knocked the

beast down, he must rapidly find a killing grip. If he fails, a strong animal could even then get away. There are two options open to the tiger. One is a nape grip: death is caused by crushing or displacing the vertebrae and severing or compressing the spinal cord. The smaller the animal, the easier such a technique becomes: with a very big (and rideable) animal the technique is a good deal harder, and can only be done by leverage, by using the victim's own weight against itself. The second option, the easier one to use against a big beast, is a throttle grip: a closing of the windpipe in the powerfully muscled jaws. One advantage of this is that a throat grip keeps a tiger out of the way of the backward threshing of the prey's antlers. The throttling of

prey is a protracted, and curiously peaceful business: some victims die with scarcely a mark upon them. Killing is a precise, not frenzied business. The big canine teeth are not only sharp, they are highly sensitive as well. The are copiously supplied with nerves, allowing the tiger to find a killing spot by feel.

Victorian hunters declared that a tiger's first act on killing is to suck the blood from its victim. But this is a misreading of the throttle grip. Quite apart from anything else, a tiger cannot suck. The structure of the lips and the jaws does not permit such a thing. A tiger's mouth is intended for killing, dismembering and slicing. A tiger is wonderfully adapted for killing, but that is not to say that its life is easy. The animals it seeks

Right:

AN ADULT MALE WITH A PAW INJURED IN A FIGHT. THIS TRIVIAL WOUND COULD BE A DEATH-BLOW: A LAME TIGER FINDS HIS HUNTING ABILITIES SEVERELY CURTAILED, AND A TIGER THAT CANNOT HUNT WILL STARVE.

are, after all, wonderfully adapted for running away or for otherwise avoiding being killed. It has been estimated by the renowned expert on animal behavior, George Schaller, that for every 20 hunt attempts a tiger makes, he will have 19 failures. Valmik Thapar, a tiger expert from India, prefers a figure of nine failures in ten attempts. But this is largely a matter of point of view: at what stage does the observer believe the tiger is fully committed to the hunt? Is giving up early, because the prey has moved on, a failure or not? The point is that killing is a difficult as well as a skilled business, and that there are many more failures than successes. The tiger, of all the cats, is the least successful hunt for hunt. This is because the tiger has chosen the most arduous role of any of the

large cats. Not surprisingly, tigers have to be capable of surviving for sustained periods without feeding. And when they kill, they gorge: they can take on awesome quantities of meat at a sitting.

A tiger, then, lives his life at constant odds of, let us say, 20 to 1 against. He is limited by many things. A tiger is consummately soft-footed, but soft, sensitive feet are a disadvantage when the ground is baked by the midday sun. Prey animals on hard, heatproof hooves will cross red-hot open ground to drink at the hottest time of day to foil their enemy. A tiger could not follow without blistering his feet. Broken and thorny ground is, for the same reason, bad hunting country for a tiger.

The tiger's explosiveness is another double-edged thing. The great power and

Above:

THE FINAL PREPARA-
TIONS BEFORE THE
CHARGE. HERE THE
TIGER'S POTENTIAL
VICTIM IS THE WATER-
LOVING SAMBAR,
INDIA'S BIGGEST DEER.

weight robs him of endurance: at the Olympic Games, gloriously muscled sprinters do not win the marathon. A tiger gets no second chance: once he has missed, he must seek another quarry - having already alarmed every beast in the neighbourhood with his charge.

Different species of potential prey animals gang up on tigers. Alarm calls cross the species barrier. Alarm is the lingua franca of the jungle: the alarm cries of deer and monkeys alike conspire to spoil a tiger's hunting. A tiger's strategy is based on the principle that no other animal knows where he is: once he is rumbled, and pinpointed by alarm calls, he must call the hunt off and start again in another place against another target.

The final double-edged weapon is both the tiger's greatest strength, and his greatest weakness. It is solitude. Lions work ganghanded, mostly in open country. They can rely on strategic cooperation, or sheer force of numbers. In this way they can kill colossal animals, and do so repeatedly. The monstrous African buffalo and hippopotamus are both targets: only a grown elephant is beyond their range. Certainly, there are great risks in attacking large and dangerous animals: but the hunting strategies of lions are designed to take risks in their stride. An injury need not bother a lion too much. It might get knocked about in a struggle with a buffalo, so much so that it cannot hunt for a while. But as long as it can keep up with the pride, it can eat while the injury heals. A tiger does not have that option.

A tiger needs to be perfect. It cannot ever rely on the efforts of others. It must take some risks with large prey in order to live: but it must control these risks as far as possible, and keep them to a minimum. The mathematics of risk - the weighing up of possible gain against possibly catastrophic injury - is something a tiger must conjure with daily. It is a difficult and precarious way of life, fraught with problems. The tiger has taken to this solitary way of life not because it is antisocial or because, like a rock climber seeking the sheerest ascent, it embraces difficulty, but because solitude is the only way of life possible for it.

The nature of the country in which tigers live makes solitude the only available option. A tiger does not live in vast open spaces teeming with herds of herbivores. Mostly it lives in forest, claustrophobic, dark, thick with cover: ambush country. The tiger must hunt by stealth, using every item of cover it can. Undergowth: thickets: trees: hollows: ravines: darkness.

Yet one of the many odd things about tigers is their willingness to break their own rules: or rather, their refusal to live in a predictable pattern. They are natural improvisers. Tigers are mainly nocturnal, just as they are mainly solitary: but that doesn't mean they lack all taste for social life, and it doesn't mean they cannot and will not operate in the day.

The habitat in most of the tiger's range does not carry large numbers of edible beasts. The prey animals are spread about the place: and that means that the tigers, too, must spread themselves out. Territorial behavior has a great deal to do with the availability of food.

Tigers move about their territories constantly. If they stay in the same small area for too long, the prey animals grow warier, and are themselves likely to move on. The alarm calls of deer, monkey, and peafowl would make life impossible. There will be several different favored hunting grounds within the territory of a single tiger.

Hunting by night involves deep and detailed knowledge of the territory. It is easy to move around your own home in darkness: you can see a pale patch of light and know at once that there is an open door, a darker patch and know that is your chair. It is hard to do that in a strange house: but in your own home,

your deep and detailed knowledge allows you to process meager information and use it in a significant way. A hunting tiger works exactly the same trick in his hunting territory.

He knows the paths, and travels by the swiftest, least cluttered routes: trails made by the passage of animals, stream beds, ridge tops, manmade roads. But he will improvise as he travels: never dogmatic, never with too rigid a game plan, always ready to improvise. A tiger knows the ways of his quarry: his way of life requires him to be a rather better naturalist than most naturalists. The seasonal and daily movements of his prey are, after all, a matter of life and death to him. He needs to know where animals feed, rest, drink.

Naturalists who study tigers have, like the tigers themselves, taken a tough option in life. The tiger's preference for solitude, thick cover and, often, for darkness, makes it one of the hardest animals in the world to observe. The various studies made by the pioneers of tiger ethology - the science of animal behavior - have all been masterpieces of patience, the result of countless thousands of man-hours of observation. One thing becomes clear: no student of the tiger is ever wholly dogmatic about the nature of his chosen beast. We have grown accustomed to stories of the marvels of the natural world: of the miraculous senses of wild beasts. Oddly enough, the tiger's sense of smell is reckoned by many to be pretty feeble. "If a tiger had to depend on its nose, it would starve to death," claims a scornful

Burmese proverb. Others rate the tiger's sense of smell very highly indeed. For a human, there is always an element of mystery about the business of smell. We smell, as it were, in black and white. Most mammals see in black and white but live in an unimaginable, highly colored world of smells.

Tigers use scent to mark their territories and for many other forms of communication. Obviously, their noses are far more sensitive than our own. They cannot fail then to use these in the hunt, even if smell is not the prime source of information. The thicker and more difficult the country, the more useful the tiger's nose becomes.

Sight is important. Tigers have a tapetum, a reflective patch in the retina which is a device for maximizing the usefulness of poor light. It is the same device that makes the eyes of dogs and cats (and tigers, for that matter) shine in the dark; human eyes do not shine. Mind you, deer have a tapetum too: a tiger is not working with any unfair advantage. Like those of most mammals, a tiger's eyes are less efficient than the human eye at giving information about shape, but very acute indeed at spotting movement. In dim light, a tiger's eyes are reckoned to be six times more efficient than the eyes of a human. Stillness is one of the great acquired virtues of jungle life, and that holds good for naturalists, predators and prey. Movement is, often quite literally, a dead giveaway.

A tiger's hearing is probably the best information-gathering device it possesses. There are many anecdotes, from hunters and naturalists, of people who have held a tiger in view, remaining perfectly still, but after a long while they make some minute, un-jungle-like click or clink - of rifle stock, or belt buckle - and the tiger is gone. A tiger can even hear a watcher breathing behind a distant screen, some say. The crack of a twig is, for a tiger, like an alarm bell: it means, as clearly as if the intruder were marching through the woods singing "We shall overcome", that a human being is about. The sounds of other animals have the reverse effect on the tiger: some say a tiger can tell the species of animal from the sound of its almost silent passage: certainly it can tell the size, where the animal is going, and what it is doing.

Tigers are by no means bigoted in their preference for night hunting. Dawn and dusk are also favored times. Often this is when prey animals are feeding and therefore, with luck, less vigilant. But no matter what time of day a tiger chooses, concealment is at the heart of every attack. The striped coat helps a motionless tiger to merge into the background, and the sharp black verticals also help to break up his outline. The black and yellow colours may on occasions look obvious to the color vision of a primate such as a monkey or a human being, but most potential victims see in black and white. The tiger, invisible and silent, waits, his plans not fixed until a possible victim is sighted.

With a potential victim in sight, the tiger next considers a line of approach: the best will take him through the best cover. If the targeted beast is moving

Right:

NIGHTVISION: IN LOW
LIGHT A TIGER'S EYE-
SIGHT IS SIX TIMES
MORE EFFICIENT THAN
THAT OF HUMANS.

Opposite:

A JOURNEY FROM THE
KILLING FIELDS: A
TIGER WILL TAKE
COLOSSAL TROUBLE TO
DRAG A KILL TO A
PLACE WHERE HE
FEELS SAFE AND
SECURE - EVEN WHEN
THE ANIMAL IS AS BIG
AS A FULLY-GROWN
COW.

from one place to another, the tiger is likely to anticipate: run ahead and seek to cut it off, an ambush rather than a stalk. If there is scanty cover, the tiger has no option but to come into the open. In full view in this way, a hunting tiger going for a sambar stag is startlingly like a domestic cat going for a bird: the same low crouch, the same hunched, taut-muscled motionlessness that can be changed in an instant into action. The approach is long and painstaking: the art of the hunt is in the preparation. The final, showy, spectacular charge is no more than the final flourish: success is the reward for patient preparation.

The final seconds before the charge have an air of almost superstitious checking and double checking: little advances and retreats of the head as the tiger makes a final assessment of distance. And then, at last, the the charge. If the tiger fails, he tries again elsewhere: another bet at 20 to 1.

Once he has killed, the tiger will move his kill to a place where he feels contented and secure. Under normal circumstances a tiger likes to make a series of visits to a kill, taking a meal each time. This can involve some herculean feats of strength. Small kills, and even quite big kills, can be carried: but big animals are also moved colossal distances and up

precipitous slopes. Some have reckoned that a tiger has the pulling power of 30 men. There are many stories of a tiger's strength: one dragged a fully grown buffalo 100ft (30m) up a steep hill; another carried away a pig that weighed 400lb (180kg). There have been measured drags of 300 yards (275m) for a big buffalo calf; other kills have been dragged 400 yards (365m) into a safe spot.

Once the tiger has a carcass before him, he will spend a lengthy period preparing it. He will bite off the tail, sometimes eating it. He will then lick around the back end before opening the carcass up. He tends to begin the meal with rump and thigh. He will then move onto the innards, eating the intestines, liver and heart, but fastidiously rejecting the rumen pouch, which is always full of

Below:

HUNTING IS A TOUGH AND DEMANDING WAY OF LIFE, BUT IT ALSO HAS ITS HIGH SPOTS. A TIGER FEASTS ON SAMBAR.

half-digested vegetation. He will not eat large bones. The eating of meat is what the tiger is built for: the carnassial teeth, just behind the canines, form a pair of scissors on each side of the mouth, and these are used for cutting through muscle and skin. This "carnassial shear" is the mark of the carnivore: bear, hyena, domestic dog and cat.

Tigers have been seen to eat up to 77lb (35kg) of meat at a sitting. A tiger works on the feast-and-famine principle, alternating gorges with lean periods between kills, but it needs an average of 15lb (7kg) of meat a day; that is what tigers thrive on in zoos. This poundage takes a lot of getting: smaller animals are elusive and swift; larger animals are wary and dangerous. It is not a simple life.

What does a tiger like to eat best? The answer is simple enough: whatever is available. The tiger has a wide range, and has lived just about all over Asia, and it has adapted, both physically and in terms of behavior, to many different habitats. Each has its own prey animals. In India and Nepal, they go for gaur, sambar, and other deer species such as barasingha, chital, hog deer and muntjac. Wild pig are taken, and tigers do not reject hare or monkey. They will also take porcupine.

This is a high risk business, because although porcupine are fairly easy to catch, they are not at all easy to kill and eat in safety. Many a tiger has died from septicemia from broken porcupine quills in the flesh.

The tiger is a killer, but it is certainly not a mad machine of destruction. It is a hard life at the top of the food chain: perhaps the hardest option in any biological system. Tigers are never wanton killers: no doubt they imagine that a chance would be a fine thing.

Tigers live their mainly solitary lives well spaced out from each other. The rationale of this is the "worst case scenario": a tiger seeks to hold a territory that will be productive enough to keep him fed even at the leanest possible times, when game is appallingly scarce and hunting is even harder than usual. The herbivore lives with food growing all around him: he has only to move his head to eat. Even when pursued by a tiger, the odds are 20 to 1 in his favour. The tiger is not a crazed killer, living ferociously in the lap of jungle luxury, killing every time the whim seizes him. In truth, he lives an almost impossibly difficult life. The tiger is a wonderfully efficient killer. He needs to be.

Right

TERRITORY PROVIDES
ALL A TIGER NEEDS TO
LIVE: SEX AND FOOD.
TERRITORIAL
BEHAVIOR IS NOT A
BATTLE FOR LAND
OWNERSHIP BUT
NECESSARY FOR
SUSTAINING LIFE.

THE FACTS
of
LIFE

SEX AND FOOD: THE BASICS OF LIFE. EVERY SPECIES OF ANIMAL, OUR OWN INCLUDED, MUST ESTABLISH A WAY OF LIFE THAT MAKES THESE THINGS ATTAINABLE. BOTH ARE REQUIRED FOR REPRODUCTIVE SUCCESS. IN DARWINIAN TERMS, THE GOAL OF EVERY CREATURE BORN IS TO BECOME AN ANCESTOR: TO LEAVE THRIVING, BREEDING DESCENDANTS, PROPAGATING ITS OWN GENES.

THE STRATEGY CHOSEN BY THE TIGER TO ENSURE BOTH FOOD AND SEX IS TERRITORY: A CERTAIN AREA WITHIN WHICH IT CAN HUNT, EAT, SLEEP, DRINK, MATE AND REAR YOUNG. TIGERS DO NOT HOLD THE TERRITORY AS PAIRS, WITH ONE MALE AND HIS MATE DEFENDING AND MAINTAINING A CHOSEN PATCH. DESPITE AN ELUSIVE AND ENIGMATIC SOCIAL LIFE, AND OCCASIONAL DRAMATIC INTERACTIONS, THEY ARE AT BASE SOLITARY CREATURES.

This has everything to do with the availability of food. Any given area of tiger habitat will be capable of providing territories for a certain number of tigers. The mechanics of tiger life do not make for large numbers of tigers who just about make do, surviving because there is just about enough prey to go round. Like all animals at the top of the food chain, a tiger needs an apparent superabundance of prey: a huge margin for error. The prey population must be big enough to allow a tiger to survive in the worst possible times. If it were not, bad times would soon kill tigers off.

That is the reason why the lifestyle of the tiger is emphatically not designed for life on the cusp of disaster. A strategy in which survival depended on the capture of the last gaur, the last sambar, would be a short term route to extinction. Instead, the distribution of tigers is based on long-term thinking. It is the social system, not the current avaliability of prey, that spreads them out over their wild habitat. The tigers themselves decide how far apart they wish to be, how great should be the margin for error.

A tiger territory needs certain important things. We must start, of course, with food and sex. A territory needs to contain sufficient prey animals throughout the year; also it needs proximity to the territory of a tiger of the opposite sex. Naturally - the word is chosen with care - the tiger's social system takes these things into account.

A tiger territory also needs access to water. The tiger evolved, it is generally thought, in the chill of the north before spreading south, and it is not nearly as heat-tolerant as the lion. Lion will often lie out in the midday sun, tongues out, lazily batting at flies, and showing no inclination at all to seek a cool place. But tigers, particularly in the warmer parts of their range, relish water and drink heavily. They also like to lie around in water, which gives relief from heat and also from the torment of flies. They will enter a pool or stream backwards, a comic but sensible maneuver, keeping the important sense organs of the head uncluttered by water. Once in there, they will often choose to lie up through the heat of the day.

An animal's territory must not be confused with human ideas of conquest and ownership. A tiger does not seek ever greater territory. A space that supplies his needs and ambitions for food and sex is all that is required. New and unfamiliar areas are, for a start, likely to be less rewarding as hunting grounds than well trodden, deeply understood places. A tiger's knowledge of his own domain is an important aspect of his hunting armory. A tiger's aim in life is not to get more than any other tiger: it is to have enough for his or her own needs, and for the needs of the offspring. In areas where prey and cover are scarce, tigers need to be more widely separated than in areas of thick jungle teeming with game. A bigger range is a sign of the poverty of the habitat, from a tiger's point of view. The prey animals occur in small numbers, widely spread. A big range reflects the poor quality of the country, not the territory-holding tiger's voracious ambition.

Left:

EVERY TIGER TERRIT-
ORY MUST PROVIDE
ACCESS TO WATER.
TIGERS LOVE WATER -
THEY DRINK HEAVILY
AND SPEND HOURS
BATHING AS AN
ESCAPE FROM THE
HEAT OF THE DAY.

Again, territory must not be confused with another human concept, the idea of property. A tiger does not own a territory. A territory is merely where a tiger has its being. What is more, a tiger's range exists in time as well as in space. The areas that two tigers use may well overlap: but the two tigers will not be there at the same time. Territories may well have seasonal fluctuations. They tend to be fluid and dynamic, shifting with new recruitment to the population of adult, territory-holding, sexually mature tigers; shifting again with the loss of such animals.

Male and female tigers have dramatically different ideas about the nature of territory. Each female will hold a small territory, adequate for feeding herself and her cubs. A male will hold a much bigger area, encompassing the territories of several females. This complex territorial arrangement is designed to ensure those simple matters of food and sex: thriving offspring, the goal of ancestorhood.

In theory, the territorial male will mate with each female in his territory when she becomes receptive and comes into estrus. But, again, one must not be dogmatic. A tiger population will include a number of transient males, sometimes subadult, but

Above:

A TIGER'S LIFE IS
DICTATED BY THE
AVAILABILITY OF PREY.
HERE A HERD OF
CHITAL DRINKS AT A
WATERHOLE IN THE
SARISKA TIGER
RESERVE, RAJASTHAN,
INDIA.

sometimes sexually mature, though not, as yet, holding and defending a territory. These can sometimes, given a lot of luck, steal a copulation. And, given even more luck, they can sometimes take over a male's sweeping, tigress-filled territory. A territory can fall vacant at the sickness or death of a tiger: a male can also challenge for a female or a territory.

It must be said that the idea of two vast male tigers tearing each other apart in the quest for a vast territory full of beautiful and eager tigresses is just about the ultimate picture of ferocity for those who believe that nature really is red in tooth and claw. And it sometimes happens - but very, very seldom. A fight may take place when two equally matched males contest for a female in estrus. That is hardly a regular occurrence: a lifestyle based on regular bouts of mortal combat is counterproductive to every individual involved. Such a struggle between two males was observed in Nepal, one male finally ousting another. But the event caused chaos in tigrine society: so great was the disruption, so traumatic the event, that no breeding took place for two years. Life could not carry on if such things happened all the time. The point is that with most territorial animals, the system is based not around conflict but around the avoidance of conflict. Many birds define their territories not by constant mortal combat, but by constant singing. The way a tiger establishes and maintains a territory is less pretty but just as peaceful, and just as effective.

It is mainly to do with urine and feces. Scent is a peripheral concern to a human: the world of smells means little more than a rough division between nice and nasty sensations. But for most mammals, scent is the radio, the local newspaper and the telephone: it is the central bureau of information and the principal communication system. Tigers leave a neverending series of "I was here" messages as they move about their territories: little notes and items of news as they pass from pace to place. This, as it were, written language of the tiger is conveyed in the literature of smell. Tigers possess anal glands which secrete a fluid that tigers can read and understand. It conveys information, not that a tiger has been here, but that this particular beast passed this way. The fluid is mixed with the tiger's urine, and it is shot backwards at various message posts, trees and leafy bushes. The odoriferous message is sprayed at the comfortable smelling height of 3-4ft (1-1.2m) from

Left:

A RARE OCCURRENCE AND AN EVEN RARER SIGHTING: TWO MALE INDOCHINESE TIGERS FIGHT OVER A FEMALE.

the ground. Males send a narrow jet, females a finer spray; obvious, when you think about it.

With lions, scent scattering is a strictly male business. Females, living together in the sisterhood of the pride, have all the communication they need within that group. Tigresses, living with cubs or alone, but always holding a personal territory, need to communicate with the world outside their chosen area. Mammals of many different species and families, when reading a scent message, characteristically perform what is called *flehmen*, a German term for a special grimacing face. The *flehmen* face is pulled when sniffing or, with some species at some times, actually tasting the urine of another mammal. At such moments they look uncannily like wine snobs savoring an intriguing vintage. The tiger is in fact sucking the scent through two holes in the palate, so that it can interpret the

Above:

MARKING THE
TERRITORY: TIGERS
WRITE A CONSTANTLY
UPDATED BULLETIN OF
THEIR MOVEMENTS IN
THE LANGUAGE OF
SMELL.

information with the aid of a sensitive piece of equipment called the Jacobson's organ.

A tiger's scent mark gives information about when the tiger passed that way, and about the sex and age of that tiger. That is useful, not to say essential information. No young transient male is going to go charging onwards, once he has found a scent mark, sniffed it, performed his *flehmen* face, and understood that 15 minutes ago a male tiger in his prime passed that very spot. He will turn and walk away, avoiding conflict. A tiger can also tell if the scent mark was made by a female in estrus. If he is the big resident male, he will seek out the female with intent: if a transient, he will have a moral dilemma to face: to risk all for the receptive female, to face the territory-holding male - or to withdraw.

Females spray far more often just before they are in estrus. Also, they will move off their chosen paths, taking many detours from a straight line, in order to make still more scent marks. They are doing more than advertising their presence in their territory: they are telling the tiger world that their period of receptivity is upon them, and that it won't last forever. Frequent scent markings become a call to action.

Tigers leave their feces in prominent places: conspicuous signposts and bulletin boards, whether you are looking or smelling. Tigers will also scrape on the ground. This is partly a stretching and suppling exercise, partly an advertisement of presence. The size and vigor of the scrape will convey information about the nature of the scraping tiger. On the ground, they use the hind legs, each leg alternately, and make parallel strips 1ft (30cm) or more in length. Some observers have noted that the scrapes are generally made in the direction in which the tiger is traveling. The tiger is then likely to urinate, and sometimes to defecate on the the scraped ground. Inevitably, the more a tiger uses a certain part of his territory, the more he or she will scrape and scent-mark there. This ensures that the tiger's favorite places, the core of the territory, is clearly identifiable by other tigers: an area where the territory holder is least tolerant of outsiders.

The tiger will also be at pains to mark the boundaries of his territory, particularly those boundaries which abut the territory of another male. Thus the scent-marking system is a major aspect of a peaceful and fruitful life. The system conveys information about how to avoid trouble, and how to find a mate. The frequency of the marking, and the numbers of individuals making the marks, will tell any transient about the tiger community of that area, and therefore give essential information about his, or less often her, chances in that part of the tiger world. If there is a dense population, and many individuals of the visitor's own sex, the area does not look promising. A less dense population, and the proximity of the opposite sex, and things are beginning to look up.

As for the residents, the markings give them information about their neighbors. Tigers live an intense social life, but at one remove, like hermits who spend their lives on the telephone. They know all about their neighbors and what they are up to. They know who they are, their age and their sex and, if with active cubs, how many. They know where their neighbors have been. Tigers will know as individuals all the tigers whose territories abut onto their own. The complex territorial patterns of males and females are all conveyed through smell. Information is constantly exchanged throughout the jungle by the silent gossip of scent. Tigers are everlastingly curious about each other, yet they seldom meet. When they do, it is mostly in order to mate.

When a female comes into estrus, all the rules of tiger life are altered. Instead of seeking to avoid each other, and moving away by easy stages when they find each other's scent marks, they move towards each other. Male tigers are reported to increase scent marking in the females' territories during their estrus. Instead of remaining silent and secretive

animals, they fill the jungle with roaring and moaning.

Zoo females coming into estrus change their behavior patterns. They are inclined to roll on their backs, rub their flanks against cage bars and rub their cheeks. They also make a puffing sound, which has another Germanic term, *prusten*. However, even when male and female have come together, zoo observers report very little physical contact before copulation. Tigers are, and rightly, very wary of each other. Both sexes are killers, and both are ferociously armed. Neither is used to the company of other adult

Below:

A TIGER PULLS THE *FLEHMEN* FACE AS SHE SAMPLES THE SCENT-MARKS LEFT BY A NEIGHBOR.

Right:

A TIGER CAN TELL THE
SEX, THE AGE, AND
EVEN THE IDENTITY OF
AN INDIVIDUAL TIGER
FROM A SCENT-
MESSAGE.

Opposite:

COURTSHIP IS A
FRAUGHT AND DAN-
GEROUS TIME FOR
TIGERS: THE FEMALE
SNARLS A WARNING
TO THE MALE AS THE
TENSIONS RISE
BETWEEN THEM.

tigers. Fully social animals have a wide vocabulary of social gestures and behavior to promote peace and appeasement. Tigers, living solitary lives, have a far more rudimentary system of social interaction. That can lead to misunderstandings and to danger. The less experienced the animal, the more touchy that animal is likely to be. Copulation, the essential part of the tiger's life, the most, if you like, natural part of life, is, in another sense, unnatural to tigers. They come together to mate almost in spite of themselves.

Very few people have witnessed tiger copulations, as you would expect from tigers' secretive lives and their taste for dense cover. But it is reported that it is often the female who takes the initiative; this is often true with lions too. It seems that a female trusts a male's amatory instincts rather more than a male trusts a female. The female has been seen offering an unambiguous invitation: she will rub flanks with her intended mate, roll invitingly before him, lick his face lavishly. A female has even been observed to mount a male, and perform a creditable mime of copulation. This stimulated the male into playing the part for real. The few copulations of wild tigers that have been witnessed contain far more physical contact before copulation than zoo tigers go in for; the lack of foreplay is, perhaps, a comment on unnatural lives.

It must be remembered that copulation is, at least potentially, extremely hazardous. A female must turn her back on the male, and expose to him the back of her neck. The neck bite is one of the tiger's favored death grips. A copulation that goes wrong can be fatal. Sparring, snarling, and batting with paws is often a part of the business: playful, even affectionate, it is still a business fraught with potential aggression and danger.

Once tigers embark on serious courtship, it rapidly becomes a honeymoon of epic proportions. For a start, the fact that a female has become sexually receptive does not mean she has actually ovulated. She will not do so until she has copulated; it may be that several copulations are required to trigger the right physiological response. Copulation is not, therefore, a one-off event. Once a couple have settled in, they are likely to be at it for days. Statistics of performance here are awesome. Strict accounting is not possible for wild tigers, but tigers in zoos have

notched up figures like 106 copulations in four days. Another figure of 52 times in a single day has been observed. Intervals between copulations are sometimes as little as 5 minutes. "It is rather amusing to see the obviously weary male being goaded into action by the female towards the end of a long mating session," said Peter Jackson, chairman of the Cat Specialist group of the IUCN, the International Union for Conservation of Nature and Natural Resources.

These statistics will impress just about everybody who is not a lion. George Schaller has counted lions in the wild copulating 157 times in 55 hours. However, the intense nature of a tiger honeymoon does emphasize the contradictory nature of the beast: a solitary animal that goes in for sustained periods of orgiastic togetherness.

Copulation itself is as brief as it is frequent: 15 to 30 seconds each time. The male may take a hold on the female by the loose skin at the scruff of the neck. This can be interpreted as passion, a need to maintain balance, or a desire to trigger a kittenish "limp reaction," as a kitten carried by its mother becomes limp and passive when seized by the

Right:

THE MALE SEIZES THE FEMALE BY THE NECK IN THE SAME WAY AS A MOTHER GRABS A CUB. THIS IS A TRADITIONAL PART OF THE TIGERS' COURTSHIP RITUAL.

THE FACTS OF LIFE

scruff. A mating tiger will often signal his climax with a roar or a moan. His next move is often to disengage as fast as he can. Post-copulatory tigresses will often whip round the second the deed is done, and slap out at the face of the male with an big unsheathed paw.

A tigress's urge to mate is so strong that if all her signals to attract a male do not bring one in to her territory, she will set out to find one. After all, it may happen that the territory holder is at the far end of his territory, perhaps even honeymooning, or perhaps some accident has befallen him. At such times the female will leave her territory and march off in search of a mate. She will scent-mark as she goes, roaring and moaning. She may call in neighboring males, or transients, in her efforts. She may, indeed, inadvertently call in two; and that is when a fight can break out.

Tigers are killers. But they do not seek peaceful existence in spite of this: they seek peace precisely because they are so dangerous, and so well armed. With the strength and the weaponry of a tiger, any resort to violence means almost certain death for at least one of

the assailants, perhaps for both. Peace is an essential part of the tiger's survival strategy: coexistence is as important as killing. A tiger cannot live without both these things.

For a tiger, killing is a profound art, one that takes years of learning. The first lessons are taught by the mother. The rearing of a tiger involves the passing on of hard-won skills. The relationship of a tigress and her cubs is as close and intense as any mother-and-offspring relationship on earth.

Above:

THE DEED IS DONE. TIGERS WILL COPULATE MANY TIMES IN A PROTRACTED, ACTION-PACKED HONEYMOON.

THE BASIC UNIT OF
TIGER CIVILIZATION:
MOTHER AND CUB.
THE LONG REARING
PROCESS ENSURES THE
CONTINUITY OF THE
TIGER'S WAY OF LIFE.

CUBHOOD

and THE RITES

OF PASSAGE

THE CIVILIZATION AND THE CULTURE OF THE TIGER ARE TRANS-MITTED THROUGH THE FEMALE LINE. THE BASIC UNIT OF TIGER CIVILIZATION IS NOT THE LONE TIGER, BUT THE MOTHER AND HER CUBS. IN TWO YEARS, BETWEEN BIRTH AND PARTING, THE MOTHER MUST NOT ONLY FEED AND CARE FOR HER OFFSPRING, BUT SHE MUST ALSO TEACH THEM HOW TO LIVE. THEY MUST LEARN THE SKILLS OF SURVIVAL, AND THE SKILLS OF SOCIAL INTERACTION. THEY MUST LEARN HOW TO USE A TERRITORY: HOW TO HUNT, HOW TO KILL. THEY MUST LEARN THEIR RIGHTS, AND THEY MUST UNDERSTAND THE RIGHTS OF OTHER TIGERS. THEY MUST LEARN EVERY POSSIBLE ASPECT OF TIGER HABITAT AND THE TIGER'S WAY OF LIFE, FOR AFTER TWO YEARS ARE UP, THEY WILL HAVE TO COPE WITH ALL THESE THINGS ON THEIR OWN.

Right:

Right:

A PREGNANT FEMALE
IS STILL MOBILE AND
ACTIVE. SHE HAS TO
BE: NO ONE WILL
HUNT ON HER BEHALF.

The tiger inherits plenty of aggressive and social instincts, but these are largely uncontrolled. A tiger needs to be taught the art of being a tiger: the only possible tutor is another tiger, and that tutor can only be the mother. She must perform one of the greatest transformations of mammalian life, a two-year-long conjuring trick that turns a blind, nuzzling and mewling kitten, a bundle of stripy fluff a few inches long, into the finest lone predator that walks the earth. It takes some doing: but the performance of that trick is the cornerstone of tigrine life.

The gestation period is short: 15 to 16 weeks. That, like most things, is a survival strategy. A heavily pregnant and waddling tigress is not going to be too efficient a hunter: and she has nobody else to kill for her. Yet for every survival strategy there is payback. Most herbivores can leap about on the day they are born:

tiger cubs, born after so brief a gestation, are helpless.

Cubs are born in small litters: two, three or four is normal. Their chances of reaching the age of two are reckoned to be about even: illness and accident, and the problems of getting enough to eat, mean that more tigers are born than can survive. That chance of surviving to breed is still lower. If that sounds wasteful or inefficient, consider that each adult breeding tiger needs only to replicate itself once before it dies for the tiger population to remain stable.

It is almost impossible to witness the birth of cubs in the wild. The tiger, secretive at the best of times, becomes doubly elusive when there are small cubs to consider. The tigress will select a safe and secure place, almost always one that makes observation impossible. Typically she selects a spot in deep cover surrounded by broken ground, or a deep fissure in a rock face. A tigress needs to feel safe and to be safe, for when she is giving birth or feeding cubs she is highly vulnerable. It is also extremely important for the cubs to be hidden, for the mother must leave them for long periods. She still needs to eat, and that means she still needs to hunt and to kill. No one else will do it for her: she remains a solitary beast. The one time a tigress will go halfway to meet trouble is when she has cubs. For once, the western mythology of the tiger has it right: the ferocity of the tigress in defence of her cubs is, indeed, an impressive thing.

So when we look for reports of tiger birth, and the early period of cub care, we are faced mainly with zoo records as a second best. Freshly born cubs mew, from 30 seconds to 3 minutes after their appearance. The tigress starts licking and drying them more or less at once. The tigress responds to the movement of the kittens: stillborn cubs tend to be ignored after one or two attempts at cleaning them.

The newborn tiger kitten needs to get hold of nourishment fairly soon after it has been licked dry. It must find and use the teat. The kittens bumble about blindly, hitting their mother at random until they at last discover the place to be. It may be that the radiation of heat from the teat is a guide. The tigress seems to do little to help the groping kitten, though she will adjust her body to make approach slightly easier.

A tigress with a first litter is far more likely to have problems than a tigress who

has done it all before. The whole business is startlingly unfamiliar to the first-time mother: she has had no practice, she has not witnessed motherhood since she was a kitten herself, and she has no older relative to model herself on. Social animals know all about young animals, which are always about, and they observe plenty of maternal behavior as an aspect of daily life. But the one thing a tigress cannot teach her female cubs is how to suckle and rear kittens. Inevitably, then, the first litter tends to be fraught with problems. The tigress is in an utterly unfamiliar situation, and may reject, refuse to feed, accidentally squash, or even deliberately kill her cubs. Kailash Sankhala, who managed a number of wildlife sanctuaries in India before becoming director of Delhi Zoological Park, reports on tigresses having their first litter in the zoo, and says that some mothers seem positively

Left:

TIGERS INVARIABLY CHOOSE WELL-HIDDEN PLACES FOR THEIR NURSERIES. AS FEWER TIGERS ARE BEING BORN IN THE WILD, MORE ARE BEING BRED IN CAPTIVITY AND, AS HERE, ARE REARED BY HAND.

frightened of the living creatures that have somehow appeared before them. They learn maternal behavior not by observation but by the expensive process of trial and error. With the second litter they tend to perform a good deal better, and by the third, they are confident, competent and caring to the point of ferocity.

The blindness of the kittens is not a technical oversight, righted by the passage of time. It is another survival strategy. It keeps the kittens static for the first few days, when they are at their most vulnerable. Blind kittens are unable to wander about, and that is just as well: wandering

Below:

TIGER MOTHERS ARE PROTECTIVE AND IMMENSELY WARY; THEY MOVE THEIR CUBS, CARRYING THEM DELICATELY BETWEEN THEIR IMMENSE TEETH, IN AN EFFORT TO KEEP THEM SAFE.

tiger kittens would be rapidly snapped up by passing predators and scavengers. Kittens grow very rapidly in the first two months of their lives, when they feed exclusively on tiger milk.

During this time the mother is often away. Hunting is a time-consuming business, and the tigress needs to eat if she is to feed the kittens. She has no pride or pack to help her. Sometimes, a tigress's entire pattern of behavior will change: she will become bolder, to a startling degree, walking into villages in search of domestic animals. At such a demanding time, risks need to be taken. For the tigress must do everything herself.

The tigress will move the kittens if she feels any concern about the chosen site: some tigresses will move ground many times. Picked up, the kittens go as limp as any domestic kittens, a little comma of fur.

The kittens have a first set of teeth at about four weeks, milk teeth that will later be replaced by the full weaponry of the tiger. By this stage they are big enough to be called cubs. But it is still likely to be several weeks before the cub tastes meat. Wild dogs will return to the den full of meat, and regurgitate to feed their pups. But a tiger's first taste of meat will be the real thing. The tigress will decide when the moment is ripe for this new stage in her cubs' life. It will normally be when she has killed close to the den. She may drag the kill, with a tiger's stunning traction power, into a preferred place first. She may feed herself before she does anything else. But then, if she is satisfied that everything is right and propitious, she will leave the carcass and go

to lead her cubs to it. And for the first time they come upon death: the vocation of the tiger.

This sets the pattern of life until the cubs are six months old: most of the time is spent waiting at the den, with regular visits from the mother, and increasingly frequent jaunts with her, to see and to share whatever it is that she has killed. They will take milk during this time, but they will also feed more and more on meat. It is a time when the tigress is away from the cubs far more often than she is actually with them, and for the cubs it is a particularly dangerous stage. They need to rest quiet and immobile for long periods, which is something they are increasingly loath to do. Meanwhile the tigress finds it increasingly hard to kill enough for all her family. She must make more and more trips, further and further from the den in all sorts of different directions.

Above:

A MOTHER MUST LEAVE HER CUBS EVERY DAY TO HUNT AND DRINK. THE CUBS MUST STAY PATIENTLY BEHIND IF THEY ARE TO SURVIVE.

Right:

A CUB INSTINCTIVELY
WANTS TO JOIN IN
WITH ALL HUNT-
RELATED ACTIVITIES,
BUT IT LACKS THE
EXPERIENCE TO DO
MUCH GOOD. HERE A
CUB PLAYS WITH A
SAMBAR HEAD.

Right:

A CUB INSTINCTIVELY
WANTS TO JOIN IN
WITH ALL HUNT-
RELATED ACTIVITIES,
BUT IT LACKS THE
EXPERIENCE TO DO
MUCH GOOD. HERE A
CUB PLAYS WITH A
SAMBAR HEAD.

When the cubs are around six months old a great change occurs. The tigress begins to take the cubs with her. They begin to learn about hunting. They begin to learn about the nature of tiger territories. It is yet another crucial period, because at first the cubs are far more of a hindrance than a help, leaping about, playing games, moving when they should be still, attracting attention and frightening the game. However, there is a payback: once the cubs are with her, the tigress can move far greater distances, and can use her entire territory at will. She is no longer limited by the need to return to the den, or by the need to kill close by the den, to give the cubs a feed. She is at last able to resume her life of purposeful wandering about her territory, once again exploiting her patch of land to its maximum. That essential aspect of tiger life is something the cubs now begin to learn.

The cubs learn stillness and watchfulness by imitation. They gradually begin to learn how to be an asset to the hunt. It is a hard lesson: when they are disruptive, failing to take the business of hunting with

sufficient seriousness, the hunting tigress will snarl in annoyance. The tiger cubs still know nothing of the art of killing, but they are very soon aware of the power they have over prey animals. They cannot kill, but they can cause fear. The prey animals do not know that the young tigers cannot kill: they cannot take the risk of assuming that any tiger is safe. That means that the young tigers can spook animals that they are quite unable to deal with. The gift of fear becomes a weapon, and they learn to use it. Mother and cubs develop a rough method of cooperative hunting. Valmik Thapar, the Indian naturalist and conservationist, has observed in Ranthambhore national park three cubs scaring deer towards their mother. He saw the same four tigers circling a herd of deer, and in the confusion they created, the mother was able to single out a deer and despatch it.

Thapar has also observed what may be a very significant part of tigrine upbringing. At one stage in India, it was common practice among tiger researchers to lure their beasts out of cover with live bait, by tethering a domestic animal in a likely spot and waiting for tigers to appear. On one occasion a domestic buffalo, instead of being tethered, was simply turned loose in an area where a mother and her cubs had been recently sighted. The tigress appeared, and at once came to a very curious decision. Instead of knocking the buffalo over, and applying the traditional neck bite or throttle grip to kill it, she merely disabled the animal with a heavy blow to a hind leg: as it were, tethering the beast herself. She then withdrew and

Left:

A TIGERCUB, 11
MONTHS OLD, IS DIS-
TRACTED FROM THE
CONCERNS OF HUNT-
ING BY THE FLIGHT OF
AN INSECT.

watched, letting her four cubs get on with the job themselves.

Two cubs approached, but the buffalo lowered his head and offered to attack. The cubs scampered off. Still the tigress watched. The cubs then tried to circle around the buffalo, but the animal responded aggressively once again and drove them off. Eventually, the biggest cub, a male, made a risky attack at the hindquarters: not the traditional point of attack for a tiger, and one inviting a kick as a counter-attack. But it worked: with the buffalo's hind leg already weakened, the buffalo could not retaliate, and the unconventional attack was enough to bring it down. A second cub joined him. After a period of shared clumsiness, the big cub sank his canine teeth into the buffalo's neck. Death-grip. In that instant, that cub came of age.

There comes a stage, after about a year or 15 months of life, when the tiger cubs become adolescents, and they start to put off cubbish things. Male cubs are more forward than females of the same age, and they become increasingly independent-minded. The cubs learn more and more about the hunt, and they do so cooperatively. But even as they learn to work as a

Opposite:

THE FAMILY UNIT IN
ITS PRIME: A MOTHER
SHARES HER TERRIT-
ORY WITH TWO MALE
CUBS, EACH 17
MONTHS OLD. IT IS AT
ABOUT THIS AGE THAT
THE PROCESS OF
BREAKING UP BEGINS.

Below:

FASCINATED BUT INEX-
PERIENCED: A FEMALE
CUB WATCHES A SAM-
BAR DEER WITHOUT
BEING TOO CLEAR
ABOUT WHAT TO DO
NEXT.

team, they live less and less like a family of kittens. They no longer seek phsyical contact with each other.

When tiger cubs grow to be more than a year old, they stop sleeping in a great furry heap. Good fellowship, which is everything to a lion, means less and less to a tiger. Each becomes more and more his or her own tiger. The sibling bond is an important fact of cubhood, binding the litter together as they lie up in wait for their mother's return, keeping them together as they follow their mother in the early expeditions of their lives. But as they prepare themselves for their solitary future, they begin to move away from

each other. This they do by a long series of easy stages: there is not a sudden and traumatic sundering of the family. Increasingly, the adolescent cubs want to be alone.

One odd thing about the rearing of cubs is that they seem to need lessons in the love of water. The tiger's affinity for water appears to be a learned rather than an instinctive response. Sankhala reports a swimming lesson. A tigress entered a patch of water, backwards according to tiger custom, and lay there in cool and comfort. The cubs approached, mystified and intrigued, but they dallied on the shore, unwilling to have anything to do with this unfamiliar stuff. One of them finally approached, with great encouraging purrs from the mother. At last it took the plunge. After a while of splashing about, the cub was deposited back on shore by the mother. The two siblings did not want to follow, so the tigress grabbed them in turn and gave them each a swift dunking.

As the cubs grow apart, they become increasingly antagonistic towards each other. Growling and snarling becomes a regular thing, particularly between the female cubs. The tumbling play fights of younger cubs are a thing of the past: instead, interactions have more than a touch of temper about them. There is now a genuine intolerance between siblings. They rear on their hind legs, often boxing with each other.

And so, again by easy stages, the adolescent tigers begin to move around the mother's territory on their own. It is generally a smallish area, and the tigers remain in close touch. But they do so less

and less by sight and physical contact and interaction; more and more by scent marking. That is how grownup tigers stay in contact: and the adolescent tigers, approaching their second birthday, are behaving more and more like grownups with every passing day. The cubs begin to kill for themselves; starting generally with small game. In India and Nepal the prey is likely to be large birds such as peafowl, or monkeys, and the fawn of deer. This is yet another critical time: perhaps the most critical time of all. The young tigers are attempting to put the long period of training into action. The next few months determine whether or not they have absorbed everything: whether they are capable of growing into effective,

autonomous predators. Their choice of prey is limited by their size, and by their limited experience and skill. They will not, at first, have a full and established territory of their own. All these make it very hard indeed to find food. It is a very serious test, and many will fail.

The tiger diaspora continues. The mother gets less tolerant of her grownup cubs, who in any case are less tolerant of any tiger's company. And so they spread further and further apart: they begin to wander away from each other. They seek prey of their own, and a life of their own. A female cub, now earning the right to be called a tigress, will leave her mother's territory. But she may not move too far from the place she was brought up. Often she

Right:

FAMILY SPATS BECOME MORE FREQUENT AS THE CUBS BECOME STRONGER AND MORE INDEPENDENT OF MIND. HERE A MOTHER CHIDES HER NEAR-ADOLESCENT CUB.

will end up holding a territory quite close to her mother's. The mother tiger will tolerate a daughter living at arm's length, and claiming an adjacent, even overlapping territory. If there is a vacancy in a female territory nearby, the daughter will certainly seek to fill it. It may be that she needs to move further away, perhaps even into sub-optimal habitat. But it is reckoned that in a given area of tiger habitat, most of the females holding the adjoining territories are likely to be related: mothers, sisters, aunts, cousins. A lion pride has much the same structure of related females: the difference is that a pride is a unit, but each female tiger is autonomous.

A male faces a much tougher future once he has moved away from his mother's territory. A male tiger's territory is much larger than a female's: therefore, obviously, there are far fewer territory-holding tigers, and far fewer vacancies for a young tiger. The male tiger has no option but to live the life of a wanderer. He must learn, and rapidly, to exploit sub-optimal habitat: the best areas will all be taken. He must learn how to cross the territory of another male tiger with care and discretion. He must learn to keep out of the way: he must learn to avoid conflict.

It is a life in the shadows: a long and hard apprenticeship, a life many times tougher than that of a young female. Only the toughest and the luckiest tigers survive it. The goal, of course, is to become a territory-holding tiger: to live a brief and glorious period as ruler of a patch of jungle, an area teeming with fat game, and packed full of beautiful tigresses. It is a desperate journey, but the prize at the end of it is immense. It is the chance of becoming an ancestor. It is the chance for the tiger to pass on his own genes. This is the goal of all life - and the pinnacle of the career of the male tiger.

Even if the life of the tiger can be reduced to such eternally relevant simplicities, that is not the full story. Tigrine life is full of exceptions and contradictions. Tigers do not necessarily keep to their own rules. The lone tiger also has a fraught and enigmatic social life in which this fierce and solitary beast shows startling gentleness and sociability.

Right

A TIGRESS AND HER
NEAR-ADULT CUBS
MEET FOR A DRINK AT
A WATERHOLE.
ALTHOUGH TIGERS
LIVE SEPARATE LIVES,
MEETINGS DO OCCUR,
AND THEY ARE OFTEN
VERY AMICABLE, EVEN
TENDER.

The
SOCIAL LIFE
of a
SOLITARY BEAST

Strife between tiger and tiger is an enduring myth. The traditional picture of the tiger is of a morose and solitary animal that kills anything that crosses its path: man, deer, fellow tiger, cub: it's all one to the secretive and sinister beast. And certainly, fights occur, sometimes to the death. These have been reported with awe and relish. So have reports of infanticide. Male tigers have certainly been known to kill cubs, and some people have concluded that a male will do so on every possible occasion. There is a truth in all these tales that revel in an imagined primeval ferocity; but it is only part of the truth.

The tales reflect the main sources of information: hunters and zoos. A hunter's main interest in an animal's behavior is tied up with his ambition of killing it. He is not interested in the beast's life apart from this, though every report of the beast's ferocity is naturally gratifying to the hunting mind. Information from zoos creates a different problem, because of the inevitable artificiality of the situation. Reports on animals in zoos are likely, in the main, to tell us more about the nature of the zoo than the nature of the tiger.

It is shocking, with the privilege of hindsight, to realize how recently most major studies on animal behavior were made. It is only in the last two or three decades that the depth and the complexity of animal behavior has been revealed. There is no short cut in this kind of work: it requires the observation of many years, often in uncomfortable circumstances. The more elusive and secretive the subject of study, the harder the work.

Major field studies of the tiger were not performed until the early 1960s. It is odd to think how sketchy was the understanding of tigers before that: how readily people had accepted the assumptions of hunters and the limited possibilities of knowledge gained from zoos. Wild tigers were pretty much a closed book before George Schaller, one of the founding fathers of ethology, published his work on tigers, *The Deer and the Tiger*, in 1967, and dispeled the myths of the unthinking ferocity of the species. In doing so, he asked the first relevant questions about the enigmatic social life of the tiger. The fact is that tigers do not avoid each other

at all costs: nor do they invariably tear each other limb from limb when they do meet. Schaller reported seven encounters between adult tigers: all of them basically benign.

Two of these took place between two females. One of these had four cubs, the other a single one. On one occasion both tigresses and all five cubs met at a kill that one or the other of the adults had made. Schaller reported that the tigresses were tense but tolerant. They each displayed aggression to the other, but they still all shared the kill. He concluded that the tiger is essentially solitary, but far from unsociable. The tiger's entire social life is based around this contradiction. Each tiger (or each unit of tigress and cubs) lives alone, but takes an almost frenzied interest in the doings of its neighbors, through the telegraph of scent markings. And when circumstances bring tigers together, they are prepared, despite their misgivings, to tolerate, perhaps even to enjoy each other's company.

Schaller added that "adults readily join for brief periods, particularly at a plentiful food supply." Charles MacDougal, an American who has made his life's work the study of the tigers of Royal Chitawan National Park in Nepal, reports a good deal of amiable interaction between tigers, most of it centering on kills. He also goes a step further, and writes of a tigress establishing what he calls unambiguously a "friendship." He adds, apologetically, that he selected the word "for want of a better term." But the apology seems unnecessary. If it were indeed nothing less than a sociable urge

Left:

A KILL IS OFTEN A
FOCAL POINT FOR
TIGER INTERACTION.
THESE OCCASIONS
CAN BE VERY TENSE
DESPITE A BASIC
MUTUAL TOLERANCE.

that brought the two tigers together on a number of occasions, the term suits tigers just as well as it suits humans.

Tigers live solitary lives not because they are antisocial, but because it is the most effective strategy for exploiting the habitat in which they live. A solitary life allows them to survive and to breed. But when circumstances are propitious - that is to say, when there is plenty of game about and killing is comparatively easy - they will be more than content in each other's company.

A kill can sometimes be a cause of strife. Theft of a kill, a cheap meal, is always a temptation, but it is a dangerous one, because tigers are inclined to defend kills. Transient males are more inclined to take risks and to seek trouble than settled animals, and they have been observed taking over kills, and willingly engaging in spats with a female for possession of the meal.

But far more often, a kill is a trigger for sociability. Tigers will often be willing to share - at least, up to a point. On these occasions, tigers tend to treat each other with great consideration and respect. Under normal circumstances a tiger will stick to the convention that a tiger on a kill has established a right over the carcass. So the second tiger, even if male, and bigger and stronger, will wait his turn. Schaller observed a large male tiger wait two and a half hours while a female and cubs ate their fill. On another occasions he

Right:

A BIG MALE SUCH AS THIS HAS NO NEED TO FIGHT; BECAUSE NO TIGER WILL OFFER A SERIOUS CHALLENGE. SUCH STRENGTH AND DOMINANCE CAN OPEN THE WAY FOR MANY FRIENDLY INTERACTIONS.

Opposite:

THE FIRST ASSUMPTION OF TIGER SOCIABILITY IS THAT THE OWNER OF A KILL HAS IMPORTANT RIGHTS. HERE AN ADULT MALE DEFENDS HIS KILL.

saw a male, hungry because "he had obviously not eaten much the previous night", meet a tigress and cubs at a kill, and leave without eating.

Tigers do not operate a dominance hierarchy at a kill, although male cubs quickly establish a dominance over their sisters. For a start, tigers do not see enough of each other to work out any formal kind of pecking order. But for that matter, lions, which spend most of their time together, never get around to working out a formal hierarchy either. Dominance among lions is a very much an *ad hoc* arrangement, and hungry lions will tug and shove and tussle for a share. Even small cubs will lash out unsheathed paws at fully-grown lions, snarling and spitting for their place.

When lions kill, they all tuck in together if the kill is big enough. It is common to see a pride all eating from the same carcass at the same time. When tigers come together at a kill, they will hardly ever eat at the same time. Lions are hurly-burly social feeders: tigers are scrupulously formal and polite. It is all part of the way a basically solitary animal avoids musinderstanding and conflict. You wait for your turn. Schaller only once observed two tigers on the same kill at the same time. It was not a happy situation, even through the kill was a buffalo, and very large. It might have been big enough to provide room for a dozen lions to feed at the same time. But with a feeding party of just two tigresses and their cubs, the atmosphere was desperately fraught.

Right:

FAMILY PARTY: A
MALE SITS A LITTLE
APART FROM THE
MOTHER, NEAREST
THE CAMERA, AND
HER TWO MALE CUBS.

The two adults spent more time snarling at each other than eating. The scene looked ferocious, for tigers cannot help but do everything on a gigantic scale. But in fact, the situation was no more tense than a couple of domestic cats rumbling and spitting at each other. No one was hurt. Eventually, the interloping tigress withdrew. However, her cub stayed. He mingled with the other cubs, ate and was tolerated.

When tigers meet amicably at a kill, they show great respect for each other's personal space. This, once again, is in marked contrast to lions, who actively seek physical contact with each other. Tigers live separate lives, and cannot know each other as pride lions do. Furthermore, every tiger is so heavily armed that any misunderstanding between tigers is potentially dangerous. Their solitary way of life makes it essential for them to substitute respect for intimacy. Tigers relate to each other in terms of formal,

one might say distinctly chilly, good manners, rather than in the warm and sloppy companionship of life in a pride of lions.

Both lions and tigers go in for infanticide on occasions. Males of both species have been known to kill litters of cubs. It has been speculated that male tigers will invariably kill cubs when they come upon them. Among lions, infanticide is generally associated with the arrival of a new male, and his taking over of a pride. Sometimes, in fact, the takeover is handled by more than one male, a pairing or even a group that will dominate the pride together. When a new male lion enters a pride, he almost always does so at the expense of another male, or group of males. The change at the top is sometimes a matter of conquest, a fight ending in the death of the dominant male; sometimes it will be because the resident has been injured or killed in other circumstances.

On taking over, one of the new male's first actions will be the mass slaughter of the cubs. The result of this mayhem is that the females who have lost cubs instantly come into estrus, and will be then be able to bear cubs by the new male. In strict reductionist terms, the newly arrived male lion is interested in propagating his own genes - not in succouring the progeny of his predecessor.

It had been suspected that tigers were far more indiscriminate cub killers: that their hostility towards other tigers extended to their own offspring. Between tigers, a meeting was mating or death: that was the thinking. Later observations roundly contradict such an idea.

Valmik Thapar observed a number of protracted nonlethal social encounters between tigers at Ranthambhore in India. Some of the encounters were sublimely friendly: almost lyrical in the way they seemed to reveal nothing less than domestic bliss. At one stage, he observed the amiable socializing of a male and female. He knew that the female had cubs, and was at once extremely concerned for them. As far as he knew, the cubs were the offspring of the male; but given the state of understanding of a tiger's family life, he feared that a meeting between father and cubs would inevitably

Left:

FAMILY LIFE IS A DELICATE BALANCING ACT. HERE, TIGERS PLAY HAPPILY TOGETHER, BUT THERE CAN ALSO BE AGGRESSION WITHIN THE FAMILY CIRCLE.

Opposite:

FACIAL EXPRESSION
AND BODY LANGUAGE
ARE IMPORTANT
ASPECTS OF TIGER
COMMUNICATION:
HERE AN ADULT MALE
OFFERS AN UNAM-
BIGUOUS THREAT.

end in the death of the cubs. There were two cubs in the family; neither was in sight. Male and female had, it seemed, come together over a sambar carcass; it was impossible to say which had killed it. Eventually, both adults withdrew from the kill and went to a small pool. Together, they entered the water (backwards of course) and rested beside each other. After they had been in the pond for a few minutes the cubs appeared. Showing neither surprise nor fear, they simply went to the pool to join their mother and the male tiger. Instead of mayhem, peace: "the tranquillity of the scene was extraordinary," Thapar wrote. "One big happy family soaking themselves in this rather small pool of water."

Thapar witnessed a number of similar amiable encounters between resident, territory-holding male tigers and the tigresses who held their smaller territories within his chosen area. He watched a series of utterly friendly responses to the cubs. He was familiar, as an observer, with three separate families of mother and cubs. With each of these families, he saw evidence of the most friendly relations with the resident male. The male would permit the female and cubs to share his kill, and would seek to share theirs: but always as a supplicant, never as a master exercising a bully's right. In each case, the male would wait his turn. He would nuzzle the cubs, and act protectively towards them.

In each case the cubs were almost certainly his own. Thapar concludes that the father takes an active role, if very much a secondary one, in providing for

his cubs and their mother. He is likely, at any one time, to have several litters throughout his territory, at various ages. His regular wanderings about his area bring him in touch with all of them. He will happily share his kill with them, and will be accepted when he asks for a share of theirs.

The chance of aggressive encounters rises steeply when male meets male. But the solution is simple, especially for the younger and weaker males: don't meet. Young tigers use the system of scent marks to keep out of the way of older and tougher tigers as much as possible. This works works most of the time: tigers are keen on preempting violence. But occasionally chance will bring male and male face to face. Even in such circumstances, it is not instant mayhem. Tigers have a vocabulary for dealing with this situation without making violence essential. Thapar reports a blood-curdling encounter between two males. Both approached each other with every evidence of ferocity: both roared loudly, unusual behavior in a tiger. They then eyeballed each other, nose-to-nose, snarling ferociously. It seemed that a fight was inevitable. But then, in an instant, it was all over. The younger male dropped to the ground and rolled onto his back. He had made himself quite helpless and vulnerable: it was a gesture of submission, a formal recognition of the other's dominance. And so at once the conflict was over. The dominant male simply walked away from the encounter, apparently well satisfied.

Tigers have a number of effective

Left:

THE SIBERIAN TIGER
IS ACCUSTOMED TO
LIFE IN THE CHILL OF
THE NORTH: HERE A
CUB WALKS OUT IN
CONDITIONS OTHER
TIGERS SELDOM HAVE
TO FACE.

Above:

THE SIBERIAN TIGER IS
THE BIGGEST OF ALL
TIGER RACES: BIGGER
ANIMALS ARE BETTER
ABLE TO DEAL WITH
EXTREME COLD.

backache knows about the imperfection of human adaptation. It is not a question of whether a design is the best it can possibly be: it is a question of whether it works well enough for the beast which possesses the design to survive, and to leave thriving young. We are all handicapped by the history of our species: humans get backache: tigers feel the heat.

But a simple question is left hanging by the theory of the northern origins of the tiger. Why does a tiger have stripes? Animals that evolved in the deep north tend to evolve colors to match the terrain. The tiger's fellow carnivore the Arctic fox is literally as white as snow. Another theory of tigrine origins, bearing this anomaly in mind, speculates on a common ancestor for lion, leopard and tiger. Each of these *Panthera* adapted to a different habitat: the lion for open plains and

savannah, where its coat is manifestly suitable for its lion-coloured lands. The leopard's spots are effective camouflage in a wide range of habitats. And the tiger's stripes evolved to match a life in dense jungle and wet, reedy areas. If this suggestion is correct, the tiger then moved north, as the ice age retreated. This theory is intriguing, but fails to explain the thickness of the tiger's insulation.

I have said that nature does not seek perfection. The tiger's need to seek relief from the climate of its most favored homeland is evidence enough for that; but all the same, when it comes to the task of hunting and killing, the tiger is about as close to perfection as any carnivore that ever evolved.

The most remarkable aspect of the tiger is its adaptability. A creature that adapts to a specialized way of life is unable to cope when conditions change. The closer to perfection a creature gets, the more limited its range of options. An animal perfectly adapted to life in the trees is lost when the trees are felled, for example. But the tiger has adapted to fill an immense geographical range, and in doing so, has learnt how to make a living in an immense range of different habitats.

The discovery that continental land masses have moved about the surface of the earth, meeting and colliding and separating and forming new groupings, was something that revolutionized all notions about the history and the spread of earthbound wildlife. And tigers spread in an impressive and bewildering fashion. When tigers were at their peak, they had a presence in almost the entirety of Asia:

almost but not quite reaching Europe: at one time there was a population of tigers in Turkey. There were also tigers all over southern and eastern China; and most surprisingly, as we have seen, in Siberia. The mixed forests of Siberia are home to a number of animals more usually associated with tropical and subtropical Asia, including leopard and dhole, the Asian wild dog.

One of the few places tigers failed to reach was Sri Lanka; by the time the tiger had penetrated into the south of India, the land bridge that once connected India and Sri Lanka had gone. The leopard was there before the tiger, and lives there still. However, the channel between Sri Lanka and the mainland is not wide: certainly swimmable for tigers, so the reasons for its absence are curious. As a further anomaly, the vultures of India have not spread to Sri Lanka either, though the island is clearly visible to a soaring vulture.

The route of tigrine expansion, it is thought, took two courses. The first led from China into Indochina and Burma, and on into India. From Burma it pushed further south still, down the Malayan peninsula, and on into Indonesia, across no longer existing land bridges. Thus the tiger established populations on the islands of Sumatra, Java and Bali. The second route went around the highlands of Tibet into central Asia, and, following river systems, went south of the Caspian Sea into Afghanistan, through Iran to northern Iraq, Azerbaijan and eastern Turkey.

As the tiger spread, populations acquired many local differences of shape, coloration and size; the shape of the skull also changed subtly from one population of tigers to another. Scientists split them into eight races, or subspecies. Thus all tigers are correctly described as *Panthera tigris*, but each tiger can also be slotted into a classification still smaller: that of race. The first race to be described, the so-called "nominate" race, has the distinction of being called tigris twice, so he can be first on the list.

INDIAN TIGER*	*Panthera tigris tigris*
SIBERIAN TIGER†	*Panthera tigris altaica*
CHINESE TIGER	*Panthera tigris amoyensis*
INDOCHINESE TIGER	*Panthera tigris corbetti*
CASPIAN TIGER	*Panthera tigris virgata*
SUMATRAN TIGER	*Panthera tigris sumatrae*
JAVAN TIGER	*Panthera tigris sondaica*
BALINESE TIGER	*Panthera tigris balica*

* Sometimes called Bengal tiger, or even Royal Bengal tiger. The prefix "royal" was added in the 1870s, when the future king Edward VII shot one in Purnea, Bihar.
† Sometimes called Amur tiger.

Many zoos have made much of their white tigers, but the white tiger is not a separate race. In fact, it is nothing more than an aberration. A freak, if you like. White tigers are not albinos; if they were, they would have pink eyes, and the eyes of the famous white tigers tend to be bluish. The freakish coloring of the coat is the expression of a recessive mutant gene. The original male white tiger was captured in the Rewa forest in India, and was kept in captivity by the Maharajah of Rewa. He mated this successfully with a normally colored female, and she

Right:

THE WHITE TIGER: NOT A TRUE RACE OF TIGER BUT A RARE FREAK, THE PRODUCT OF A RECESSIVE GENE.

Opposite:

THIS INDOCHINESE TIGER LIVES IN CAPTIVITY. HE IS NEAT AND SLIGHT, AT LEAST WHEN COMPARED TO THE GIANTS OF SIBERIA. HE IS ALSO DARKER, AND MORE NARROWLY STRIPED.

produced three litters of normally-colored cubs. A female from the second litter was then mated to the father: she gave birth to four white cubs, and thus white tigers were established as a zoological curiosity. This is all interesting enough genetically and, for that matter, occasional wild white tigers have been seen in the the Rewa forests, but it doesn't really have much to do with the natural history of the tiger. There are more important things to do with tigers than to breed them like show dogs.

What matters far more are the differences between the true races of tiger. The principal difference between the northern tigers and those of the south is not a hard one to spot: size. Following the "polar bear" principle - technically called Bergmann's rule - the Siberian tigers, which live in the cold, are effortlessly the biggest. Claims for the biggest tiger ever shot are impressive, but open to a little doubt. A figure of 13ft (4m) in length and 700lb (215kg) in weight is claimed; there are even more spectacular claims for 4ft (1.2m) high at the shoulder and 800lb (245kg) in all. But hunters, always a record-seeking class, have argued

endlessly as to whether a tiger should be measured in a straight line from nose to tail, or whether the tape should follow the contours of the body; thus a hunter's measure of a tiger's size is not completely reliable. As for weight, a tiger can easily carry 50lb (23kg) of meat in its stomach, and the questions of whether or not this is included throws further doubt on the more spectacular claims.

Indian tigers are around 10ft (3m) in length, 400-450lb (180-205kg) in weight, for the average male. Further south into Indonesia, the tigers are smaller, closer to

Right:

THE INDIAN TIGER IS
THE NOMINATE SUB-
SPECIES, AND SO HAS
THE HONOR OF BEING
CALLED *PANTHERA
TIGRIS TIGRIS*.

9ft (2.7m) in length. They are darker and more narrowly striped than Indian tigers, with slightly shorter fur; the Siberian, in contrast, has a long and shaggy coat. To generalize, the further north, the larger, paler and shaggier the tiger is; the further south, the smaller, darker and more scantily furred.

The Siberian species lives in the sort of country that would be unrecognisable to the Indian tiger. Though its life of ambush is basically the same as any other tiger, it has adapted to a life among thickets of birch, scrub oak and walnut. The crucial tree is the Korean pine, which drops large seeds. The seeds are very attractive to wild boar, which are the Siberian tiger's staple prey. Tiger tracks have been found in deep snow and in temperatures of -30°F (-34°C). The Chinese tiger hunts in oak and poplar forests, and thickets of grass; and also in coniferous forests further south. The Caspian tiger adapted to lowland reedbeds, and the cork oaks of that region's mountainous country. The Indian tiger can adapt to just about any kind of forest the subcontinent can come up with: deciduous, evergreen, dry, humid, and thorn forest. They have even adapted their behavior to a life among mangrove swamps, where they exist as semiaquatic creatures. On the southern slopes of the Himalaya, they have been recorded as high as 13,000ft.

In short, the tiger is an immensely versatile beast. Given some prey and some cover, it will adapt its behavior and its lifestyle to fit: over the millennia, it will also make minor adjustments in size

Left:

THE SUMATRAN TIGER
IS DARKER IN COLOR
THAN THE INDIAN
TIGER, WITH
NARROWER STRIPES,
AND AVERAGES HALF
THE WEIGHT OF THE
SIBERIAN TIGER.

and shape. From one end of Asia to the other, from the heights to the low-lying swamps, extreme cold, extreme heat: there is nothing you can't throw at a tiger. It is one of nature's great survivors.

But three of the eight races of tiger have somehow failed to survive. The Caspian tiger, the Javan tiger, and the Bali tiger are all extinct. The Bali tiger went in the 1940s; the Caspian tiger went in the 1970s, the Javan tiger most probably in the 1980s. Extinctions are coming at us faster and faster.

What has changed, then, after all these millennia, to make the existence of three races of these adaptable, versatile, and supremely effective beasts impossible? It is

at this stage we must introduce the villains of this piece. He, and she, have the potential to turn things around, and to become, in a dramatic last-act *coup de théâtre*, the hero and the heroine: the friend and the saviour. All it will take is the reversal of history.

The relationship between humans and tigers is as complex as it is contradictory. Tigers seize the imagination: of individuals, of societies, of cultures. Tigers have been worshipped; tigers have been slaughtered. The peoples of both east and west have been enriched by the tiger; it is part of human history, of human thought.

THE SOUL
of the
STRIPED ONE

In every culture where the tiger is to be found, humans have regarded it with a bewildering mixture of fear and respect, love and loathing. Tigers are seen as embodiments of both good and evil. Fearsome beasts committed to peaceful interactions and the avoidance of trouble, they really are eternally baffling creatures. Perhaps not to themselves: but certainly, humans have always found them so.

In previous centuries, in less humanly crowded, more tiger-filled days, the people who lived in or near the forests of Asia had, as a central concern of life, the need to come to terms with the tiger. Understanding nature, and the place of a person and a community in nature, is a central need of rural people - all the more so when nature is most spectacularly represented by so uncompromising an animal as the tiger. And so, in such communities, one of the first steps towards reaching an understanding of life, and of death, was to come to an understanding of the tiger.

The essential thing was to find a way of coping with life alongside tigers. Coexistence was, after all, the only possible option. Wiping out the local population of tigers was, in the days before firearms, mechanized farming and tree felling, an impossible idea and one that simply would not occur to a village cultivator. They had to accept tigers as a natural, an inevitable and an inescapable part of life. If life was to continue in some sort of harmony and peace of mind, people and their communities had to come to terms in their own minds with the striped killer of the woods.

To come to terms with nature is the first concern of all pre-industrial people. It is not easy to grasp this: for most of us, industrialization, rising population and the ever greater intensification of agriculture has changed the way we look at nature, and the way we understand our fellow animals. Tigers became pests and enemies in the eyes of people whose ancestors had respected and revered the animal. Decision makers in the cities oversaw the loss of tiger habitat and the remorseless persecution of tigers. Ancient, ancestral superstition and sentimentality about tigers seemed outdated nonsense: a relic of the primitive past from which Asia was fighting to free itself.

Now the second wave has set in. Ever greater industrialization is no longer seen as a universally unquestioned good, and the need for conservation is daily more obvious. There is a growing realization of what has been lost. These lost things include many tigers, yes, and much tiger habitat, but more than that: people have also lost the the human desire to live in harmony and understanding with their fellow mammals and with nature.

The mythology of the tiger pervades Asia, just as bears and wolves pervade the fairy stories and myths of northern Europe. Tigers pop up here and there in Hindu mythology, they lurk in Chinese horoscopes, they break from cover in exercise and combat forms. The more ancient the beliefs, the more the important the tiger becomes. When you come to animistic systems, ancient beliefs based around the understanding of natural forces, you see the extent to which the tiger once dominated Asian hearts and minds. From all this it is clear how important a part the tiger still plays in Asian thought.

The central part of all animistic beliefs about the tiger is not the myth of the the tiger's ferocity. It is the fact. People who live closely with tigers can never escape from the fact that tigers kill people. No

philosophy or system of beliefs that fails to take in this essential fact of life, or death, is worth a button. The ferocity of tigers is an ineluctable fact of daily life. How many has it in fact claimed? One guess, but really no better than a guess, says that in the past 400 years tigers have killed 1 million people; that works out at 2,500 a year. As recently as 1979, police in a province of Sumatra produced figures to demonstrate that the tiger could even beat its great rival in destruction, human beings, when it comes down to straightforward killing. They said that in a year 30 people were killed by tigers; but only 25 people were murdered by other people.

The very idea of assessing figures for tiger killings is surrounded by problems. It is far easier to blame a tiger for the loss of missing and murdered people than to search for the victims or their killers. As a passing thought, it is worth noting that while tigers are considered as purely ferocious and elephants utterly benign, elephants kill 200 to 300 people a year in India alone.

But tigers are ever ambiguous, never enemies through and through. Tigers may be fearful, and naturally they kill people. But they also kill such renowned crop raiders as deer, wild pigs and monkeys. That means that a tiger can be welcomed and feared at the same time. His presence

Above:

THE FISHING FOLK OF THE SUNDARBANS HAVE MAN-EATING TIGERS AS THEIR NEIGHBORS. THEY PRAY TO THE GODDESS BANA BIBI, WHO PROTECTS THEM FROM THE BEASTS OF THE JUNGLE: THE RELATIVES OF THOSE ENTERING THE JUNGLE IMPLORE HER WITH COCONUTS AND FLORAL OFFERINGS TO ENSURE THEIR SAFE RETURN.

Below:

THE ROYAL BENGAL TIGER OF SUNDARBANS. THE PEOPLE OF THIS AREA MUST COME TO TERMS WITH TIGERS THAT ARE ENORMOUS IN SIZE AND HAVE THE TRACTION POWER OF 30 MEN. IN THE BENGAL SUNDARBANS ALONE, TIGERS HAVE KILLED AT LEAST 430 PEOPLE IN THE LAST 21 YEARS.

near a habitation will frighten these hungry animals away from cultivated fields. It is an extension of the keeping of a cat to catch rats: the price of an occasional cow to the tiger is often regarded as a fair one for the tiger's guarding of the crops.

Traditionally tigers have inspired as much respect as they have loathing. The Kerinci people of Indonesia have, far back in their culture, both feared and respected, admired and distrusted the tiger. Such ambiguities and ambivalences change and change again - but at base the

tiger is seen a good animal, even a just one. The Kerinci people have a myth that concerns an agreement on demarcation: the forest for the tiger, the cultivated lands for humans.

Some Kerinci myths speak of the tiger's origin, and his siring by a staggeringly potent human. The line between tigers and humans is, in culture after culture, vague and shaky, and what is more, infinitely crossable. The tiger, thus sired, was at first friendly, but later grew unruly, and began killing livestock. So the agreement was made, the lines of demarcation were drawn up, and the two sides promised to respect each other's territory and to refrain from disturbing each other. It was emphatically a gentleman's agreement.

The tiger is essentially a moral animal. But no mythology is a straightforward business, and this truism seems to count double where tigers are concerned. The Kerinci people differentiate between "spirit tigers" and "real tigers". Good, kind, righteous spirit tigers defend the villagers and their livestock from real tigers, and stop them from too frequent raids on livestock. What is more, spirit tigers will guide humans who get lost in the forest.

It is this demarcation between forest and cultivation that lies generations deep in many Asian minds. Western minds know something of the same split: a division that develops more strongly with the destruction of wilderness. The more ancient the culture, the more precarious the division becomes. In many of the animistic systems of Asia, it is believed that wild animals are herded by the spirits of the forest, just as humans tend their own domestic beasts. The forest represents the mysterious, the ambiguous, the difficult, the hidden: it is the domain of spirits and souls. Such beings must be treated with great respect: good manners and correct protocol are vital when dealing with forests. It seems that Western civilization has passed through three thousand years of progress in order to return to this very conclusion: that forests and the beings that live there deserve respect and consideration.

Most animist systems believe strongly that you should never speak disrespectfully of tigers. Many go further: you should not actually refer to the tiger by name. For a start, the tiger may answer to his name: instead, he is referred to as hairy-face, the striped one, grandfather, or lord. Different communities have different taboos. Some warn against the dangers of acting in a "tigerish" way. You must never walk on all fours, eat from the pan, or take a wooden pestle into the garden. The last one sounds a trifle odd, but a pestle is associated with a tiger's tail. The thinking behind these apparent oddities is as sound as a bell. The more you respect the tigers and their forest, the more likely you are to be free from their wrath.

But both sides are capable of breaking the rules of demarcation, of upsetting the delicate, ever precarious balance of coexistence. A tiger that does so, that takes livestock, that kills a human, is likely to find that its life is forfeit. Coexistence is not always easy; however, coexistence is

seen as essential. That too is a conclusion that sits well in modern terms.

Many systems of belief discourage the killing of the tiger, in ever present fear of exciting the wrath of all tiger-kind. Traditional Sumatran beliefs prohibit the killing of a tiger, except in self-defence, or immediately after the tiger has killed a friend or a relation. In *The Golden*

Above:

THE HINDU GOD SHIVA HAS A CLOSE RELATIONSHIP WITH TIGERS. IN ONE STORY A TIGER IS THROWN AT HIM BUT HE TRANSFORMS IT INTO A STRIPEY LOIN CLOTH. THIS IMAGE SHOWS THE DANCE OF SHIVA.

Bough, J.G. Frazer says that when Europeans set a trap for a tiger, local people of Sumatra go to the forest to explain that they did not set the traps, nor even consent to their setting. Frazer also cites traditional Bengali people, who will kill a man-killing tiger: but once it is slain, they will explain to God that the killing was in retaliation for the loss of a kinsman, and that they will never slay a tiger again - at least, not without similar provocation.

Ancient animistic beliefs blur the distinctions between humans and animals. The distinction that seems blindingly obvious to city man is not half as obvious to the the people of the land, to people who live in or by the forest. For the people of the cities, far too worldly and sophisticated to share belief in such things as spirit tigers, believe that people are people, and that animals are animals: nothing to do with them at all. The fact that people are mammals, and share, among other things, a common ancestor with the tiger, is never considered. Once again, traditional beliefs possess truths that modern people have mislaid. It is the ancient beliefs that have a modernity and an urgency that leaves smug assumptions about human convenience looking foolish, illogical, unscientific and out of date.

It is a matter of souls. People, other animals, all living things, have souls; so do many nonliving things. Sometimes they possess more than one soul. It is a confusing, shadowy business, determinedly elusive of understanding. For souls are not fixed items: they move on at death, but not only at death. Souls can move, on occasions, from body to body. When considering matters of this kind, you inevitably find that the tiger, or if you prefer, the tiger's soul, plays a huge part in this world of shadows. This question, for example, has vexed many Asian communities: what happens to the soul of a person who is eaten by a tiger? Some say the person eaten becomes the soul of the tiger. Others say that the victim rides the tiger's back. Some say that the possession of a tiger by this new soul is a good thing, others a bad thing,

others still, find it a deeply ambiguous business.

For a soul is the deepest essence of a living or unliving thing; it follows, then, that the greatest power attainable is power over souls. In many cultures the power of a magician is demonstrated by his ability to move his own soul into another body. Magicians turn themselves into animals. Clearly, a magician who can turn himself into a tiger is as powerful a person as you could find. In some places it is believed that magical powers are bestowed on humans by the master tiger of the forest. Traditionally, magic comes from the forest: it is there that the spirits live. In the forest is mystery, and the multi-souled creatures that live far beyond common human understanding.

The man-tigers of Asia have obvious parallels with European traditions of the werewolf: the man who becomes wolf. Belief in "weretigers" is, or was, particularly strong in peninsular Malayasia. At spirit seances a magician will assume tigrine movements. If healing is the object, he may lick the body of his patient and growl.

Weretigers are difficult and dangerous but, as a further aspect of the ambiguity of everything to do with tigers, even weretigers can be helpful to less powerful beings. There is even a rather pleasing tale of a tiger in Vietnam, an animal that was said to be inhabited by the spirit of a deceived husband. The tiger preyed only on women. Its presence prompted a great outbreak of marital fidelity in the village.

It is clear that the mysteries of the spirit world, the mobility of souls, and

the various forms they take, including that most fearsome form of all, that of the tiger, play a strong part in maintaining social order. McNeely and Wachtel declare in their book *Soul of the Tiger*, "These powerful links with the spirit world provide strong elements of social control and cohesiveness... with so many spirits and souls wandering around like

Above:

DURGA, A FEARSOME ASPECT OF THE HINDU FEMALE DEITY, IS TRA-DITIONALLY SHOWN, AS HERE, RIDING A TIGER.

Right:

AN ILLUSTRATION FROM THE 13TH-CENTURY TEXT *VARRNAROBA JATAKA.* THIS WAS ONE OF THE FIRST BUDDHIST TEXTS FROM BURMA. THE LION AND THE TIGER ARE GOOD FRIENDS AND LIVE IN A MOUNTAIN CAVE IN A FOREST. A GREEDY JACKAL TRIED TO MAKE THEM QUARREL BY TELLING THEM THAT EACH MALIGNED THE OTHER. THE JACKAL HOPED TO MAKE THEM KILL EACH OTHER SO THAT HE COULD EAT THEM, BUT THEY DID NOT LISTEN TO GOSSIP.

Opposite:

THE TIGER PERMEATES TIBETAN FOLKLORE. HERE THE TIGER IS BEING TRICKED BY THE HARE, IN A TALE ENTITLED "HOW THE HARE GOT HIS SPLIT LIP".

undercover cops in unmarked cars, people are encouraged to behave strictly according to the norms of their society."

Some beliefs go further than this. Tigers are instruments of divine retribution. A person is killed by a tiger because he or she has erred, and must be punished. Sometimes this means the breaking of tribal rules. It is a pervading belief that the tiger is worthy of respect: the Moi tribe calls him "the gentleman;" much as the Furies of the classical world were courteously termed the Kindly Ones, the Eumenides, a form of cosmic politness intended both to show proper respect to these bringers of disaster, and to forestall their anger.

But not all Asian cultures see tigers in an equally gentlemanly fashion. In Java, and in some aspects of Hindu mythology, the tiger denotes blind fury and untrammeled sexual passion. The androgynous Hindu god Shiva is sometimes depicted with a tiger's face, sometimes also wearing a tiger skin. In one Hindu myth, a tiger is used as a weapon. Shiva is pelted with all kinds of fearsome things: fire, snakes and a tiger; but Shiva converts all the weapons into benign objects, bracelets, and a striped loincloth.

Tigers also figure in some Hindu mythologies of the origin of evil. The god Indra was involved in the theft of a drink, *soma*, which he consumed: parallels with the Garden of Eden need little stressing here. But the result of Indra's crime were

Right:

THE CHINESE GOD OF WEALTH IS ALWAYS ASSOCIATED WITH THE TIGER - WHAT BETTER ANIMAL, AFTER ALL, TO GUARD YOUR TREASURES? THUS THE TIGER'S FEROCITY BECOMES AN AUSPICIOUS THING.

far more instantly dramatic than Adam and Eve's trangression. At once, dreadful substances flowed copiously from Indra's body, enough to pollute the entire world with evil. A lion sprang from the fluid that escaped from his nose, a jackal from his ears, and from the lower bodily openings sprang tigers and other wild beasts. Here, then, the tigers have little ambiguity. The myth makers here have moved a long way from the respectful animistic soul watchers of the forests.

The tiger, predictably enough, also has a busy role to play in many traditional stories and myths, as king of the beasts. Like the lion, in many tales more familiar to the western mind, the tiger represents royalty, wealth and power, as well as ferocity, fearlessness and wrath. The tiger

has always been treasured by Kshatriyas, the warrior caste of India; the tiger is their symbol and inspiration. This represents yet another example of the strong sense of identification between people and tigers. Shiva, as we have seen, wears a tiger skin when he is depicted in his destructive aspect; Durga, an aspect of the female principle and the wife of Shiva, actually rides one.

Hinduism is the religion of a million gods: there is God, or a god, in everything. William Blake, the English poem and author of the greatest tiger poem of them all, "Tyger! Tyger! burning bright..." declared unambiguously, "Everything that lives is holy." That is a line that helps the Western mind come to terms with the vast extent of Hindu mythology. The living tiger is clearly holy to the devout Hindu.

Buddhism, a religion which first arose in India, lists the tiger in a group known rather charmingly as as the Three Senseless Creatures. The tiger represents anger; his colleagues are the monkey who stands for greed, and the deer, which represents lovesickness.

The tiger has always been an important part of Chinese mythology: a privilege that the tigers have paid for very dearly, as we shall see in in a later chapter. For the Chinese, the tiger has always been the king of the beasts and the lord of land animals, and it is much associated with military might. It was considered, at one stage, one of the four auspicious creatures.

The Chinese god of wealth rode a tiger, the better to guard all those money chests. That makes the tiger the emblem of the gambler, a type not exactly unknown among the Chinese. But Chang Tao-lin, an early and central figure in Taoism, is often drawn riding a tiger: here the tiger represents not ferocity but authority. Once again, the tiger's ambiguity leaps out at us.

The tiger is also one of the twelve beasts of the Chinese horoscope. A person born in the year of the tiger is said to be born lucky - which is just as well, because tiger people, by nature, take tremendous risks. Tigers are sensual, restless, and unpredictable: enthusiastic and impulsive, often hell to live with.

Tigers are part of Asia's heartbeat: part of the spirit and the soul of a vast, diffuse, and baffling continent, full of a thousand differences, not to say contradictions, of belief and custom. If you turn your attention to just about any aspect of Asian life, a tiger will jump out at you. Asian libraries are seething with tigers: *The Tiger Kills: India's Fight in the Middle East and North Africa*; *The Springing Tiger: Story of a Revolutionary*; *Riding the Tiger: The Politics of Economic Reform*. Any one who seeks a symbol or a strong image for anything to do with Asia turns to the tiger.

Tigers have lurked in the Asian mind for countless generations. They are to be found in the near-incomprehensible - to a westerner - complexities of Hindu myth, and in the subtle and bewildering nuances of Chinese symbolism. Half easy to comprehend, yet wholly baffling to the analytical mind, are the vaguer myths of the animists: dark stories of dark jungles where the souls of people and of tigers inhabit so strange and elusive a common ground: sharing bodies, sharing souls, sharing the secrets of a dark world.

The tiger lives on in in a thousand myths. It dominated Chinese mythology: now the Chinese tiger is itself a more or less entirely mythical creature. There are scarcely more tigers walking the wilds of China than there are dragons. If we are not careful, future generations will have no reason to believe that tigers were ever any more real.

Right:

WITH NO EXPERIENCE
OF THE TIGER IN ITS
NATURAL
ENVIRONMENT, THE
WEST'S IMAGE OF THE
BEAST WAS BASED
ENTIRELY IN THE
IMAGINATION.

BOUNCING *and*

BURNING

BRIGHT

In Asia the myths of the tiger are based on a real animal: an animal that was and in some places still is a daily part of many people's lives. The West has mythologized the tiger on its own account, but with one important distinction. In the West the tiger was pretty well a mythical animal: never a part of daily experience and no more real, as far as most people were concerned, than a dragon. But as with all stories and myths about wild animals, the West's understanding of the tiger reflects all sorts of beliefs and assumptions about the relationship between human beings and nature.

Orthodox medieval thought was absolutely unshakable in upholding the perfect centrality of human beings in the cosmic scale of things. The earth was the centre of the universe, human beings were the crown of creation, and every other aspect of life demonstrated the glory of God, and his eternal thoughtfulness in providing for the most favored of his creatures.

The medieval bestiaries were a kind of moral wonderland: books containing account after account of wild beasts. Myth, natural history, and moral instruction were not separate matters. All were aspects of a grand, unified cosmic view, it being self-evident to the medieval mind that the proper study of mankind is God. Thus animals that could be eaten represented God's bounty. Other animals were there for spiritual nourishment and edification: in one of the many extraordinary pieces of mythologizing, the pelican was said to feed her young by stabbing herself, on the breast, and feeding her young on the blood that fell; thus the pelican was a living allegory of Christ: the self-sacrificing savior.

Tigers occasionally pop-up in bestiaries, along with almost equally-mythical lions. These mega-carnivores were generally used to represent the ferocity of nature: a humbling device to keep man in his proper place. And across the centuries, tigers have held onto their place as emblems of perfect ferocity, the more so for being so little known.

Tigers also turn up occasionally in heraldry, as emblems on shields and banners. They are generally referred to by the

borrowed French name of "tigre." Heraldic tigers, being no better known to heralds than they were to the compilers of bestiaries, were much stylized beasts. The tigre tended to be shown with a rather wolf-like body, with short, powerful and massive jaws set with massive canine teeth, recalling the tiger's non-ancestor, the sabertooth. However, the tigre departs from usual tigrine customs at the end of his snout, where he is adorned with a large curved horn. He carries tufts of hair on the back of his neck, and is finished off with a lion's tail: a truly mixed-up beast. His heraldic job was to symbolize ferocity, strength, cruelty and destructiveness.

This ferociously, extravagantly armed version of the tiger accorded with visions of nature as basically hostile. Humans were seen seen as perpetually fighting against nature: survival was a hard task in a hostile world. The subduing, the taming of nature was the clear and obvious duty of humankind. It seemed a task that was next to impossible.

Western people sought not harmony with nature, but control. They wanted nature caged, tamed, understood. By the eighteenth century, much of the English landscape was manmade: tamed and controlled by agriculture. Control was a sign of civilization. The great parks of aristocrats were completely designed: they represented landscape architecture, and were emphatically the work of man: "artful wildness," in the phrase of the poet Alexander Pope. Pope also wrote, in his Epistle to Richard Boyle, Earl of Burlington, of what land was for:

> ...rising Forests, not for pride or
>   show,
> But future Buildings, future Navies
>   grow:
> Let his plantations stretch from
>   down to down,
> First shade a Country, and then
>   raise a Town.

The tiger was a symbol of all that civilized life rejected. The tiger represented not control but its loss. The tiger stood for both nature out of control and it also stood for human nature out of control. It embodied the darkest impulses of human beings; it represented the dreadful animal nature that lurked in civilized humankind, something that needed to be suppressed if civilization was to continue. The tiger hinted at the dreadful truth: that *Homo sapiens* is a mammal, kin to *Panthera tigris*.

It was William Blake who rehabilitated the tiger. Blake gave us the most famous tiger in Western literature, the subject of his poem in *Songs of Experience*. The poem is about ferocity, but Blake illustrated it

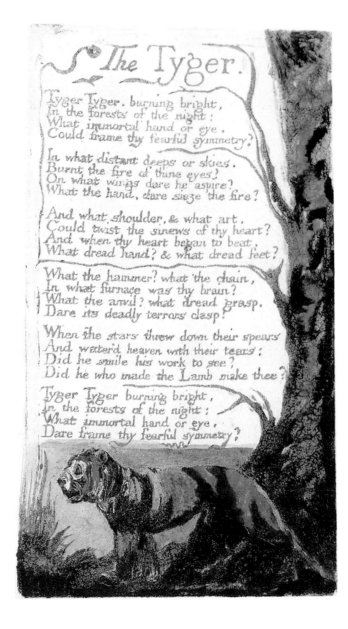

Below and opposite

WILLIAM BLAKE REP-
RESENTS HIS BEATIFIC
VISION OF PEOPLE IN
HARMONY WITH
WILDLIFE AND WITH
THE WILDNESS OF
THEIR OWN NATURES.

himself with a tiger of gloriously teddy-bear-like qualities. The last two stanzas of the poem are rather less huggable:

> When the stars threw down their
>   spears,
> And water'd heaven with their tears,

> Did he smile his work to see?
> Did he who make the Lamb make
>   thee?

> Tyger! Tyger! burning bright
> In the forests of the night,
> What immortal hand or eye
> Dare frame thy fearful symmetry?

The key question is whether the God who made the lamb could also make the tiger. Blakes's poem dealt with the contradictions of divine, and also of human nature: lamblike qualities abound in humans, just as tigrine qualities do. Blake was cutting against the grain of conventional "civilized" thinking about nature and the place of humankind. Blake did not believe that nature must be tamed if it is to be worth anything: he did not believe woods were there to build warships. Blake valued wildness, both in wilderness and in human nature. That is what his burning tyger is about.

Blake returns to the same theme on countless occasions: the tiger often turns up to add his ferocious emphasis to the thought, though never as dramatically, as perfectly, as ferociously or like a teddy-bear as he does in "*The Tyger*". In his poem "*The Little Girl Found*", the lost child's sorrowing parents at last

> "saw their sleeping child
> Among tygers wild.

> To this day they dwell
> In a lonely dell;
> Nor fear the wolvish howl
> Nor the lion's growl."

This is as joyful an acceptance of wild nature as you can get. Blake returns to tigers in his *Proverbs of Hell*, which is a series of declamatory epigrams full of life-affirming wisdom and hot challenges to conventional thought. After declaring, among other things, that "The lust of the goat is the bounty of God," Blake tells us: "The tygers of wrath are wiser than the horses of instruction." Thus the tiger is a symbol of natural force, and natural force, he decrees, is a wonderful and positive aspect of human nature - and for that matter, of any other kind of nature. In natural, unspoilt things were purity and wisdom: tigers and lambs are eternal contradictions, esssential to each other and to human life. The tiger was, briefly, a hero.

However, even as Blake was writing, the British Empire was growing: and India was well on the way to becoming the jewel in the Emperor's crown. And if India was the greatest prize of Empire, the greatest prize a servant of the Empire could hope for was a tiger. Hunting, in the sense of gleeful destruction of life, for fun, for "sport," not for food, had long been part of Western life, and it still is. You ask an English fox, or a French thrush, or a Sicilian honey buzzard, or anything at all that is foolish enough to show a feather over Malta.

The shooting of tigers was seen as the greatest sport of all. No animal is so colossally ferocious: no animal could possibly be more gratifying to its killer's self-esteem. Tiger shooting was fun, but it was seen as far more than fun by the hunters themselves. Hunters saw themselves as angels of light and mercy,

freeing a dark foreign land from primeval terrors. They were killing the dark side of nature: they were aiding the advance of civilization. They were seizing control for humankind. A hunter called, bizarrely enough, H. Shakespear, wrote in 1860 about the slaying of a pair of tigers that were, he says, maneaters: "It was much that I had been the avenger, constituted by Him, who ordains all things, to slay these tigers and to save further loss of life." Another hunter, E.H. Baker, wrote a few years later: "There are persons whose minds are so ill-balanced as to regret the present paucity of tigers ... even the

Right:

TAMING THE WORLD: THE UNTRAMMELLED FEROCITY OF NATURE AND FOREIGN PARTS IS BROUGHT UNDER CONTROL BY THIS FINE SPECIMEN OF WHITE VICTORIAN MANHOOD IN A PICTURE ENTI- TLED "A TIMELY RESCUE" BY STANLEY BERKELEY.

most morbid mind must allow that the country and people are better for the absence of tigers."

As hunters continued on their self-applauding way, they somehow developed the myth of the tiger as coward. As hunting increased and spread - one hunter wrote that "every tiger in India has been hunted" - tigers got better and better at keeping out of hunters' way. The tiger was rejecting chances to be executed; therefore the tiger was a coward.

One of the greatest tigers in literature, and by far the most cowardly, is Shere Khan of Rudyard Kipling's *The Jungle Book*. Shere Khan, the Lame Tiger, is an unrepentant mankiller, who claims as his right the life of a human child. But the child is adopted by wolves and accepted by the wolf pack. Shere Khan is denied. But ten year's later, when the child is half grown, Shere Khan returns, and turns the pack against Mowgli, the wolf-child. Mowgli fights off the entire pack, using fire as his weapon, and singes the Lame Tiger himself. The tiger is turned back by man's mastery of fire.

Mowgli then goes to the world of men, and works herding the buffaloes. But he returns to the jungle to kill Shere Khan, luring him to a ravine, and splitting his herd in half: sending the bulls in at one end, the cows and calves at the other. The Lame Tiger is trampled to death, and Mowgli has won his war. It is a sad and terrible victory: Mowgli returns to the village, but the villagers turn on him. "Man-pack and wolf-pack have cast me out," says Mowgli when it is all done. "Now I will hunt alone in the jungle."

Left:

MOWGLI'S FIRST VIC-
TORY OVER THE LAME
TIGER, SHERE KHAN,
IN *THE JUNGLE BOOK*
"THUS AND THUS,
THEN, DO WE BEAT
DOGS WHEN WE ARE
MEN."

The Jungle Book, and its less read, equally compelling sequel, *The Second Jungle Book*, get stranger with every reading. Partly, the tales are about humans and nature: about civilized life and the life of the jungle. The jungle has laws and patterns and a civilization of its own: one that works, it seems, far better than the civilization of humans - as long as everybody obeys its laws. But the jungle is not a place of mindless conformity: it can take in its stride a thousand oddities: even the arrival of an outsider like Mowgli.

In some ways, the wolf-pack represents order and civilization: they call themselves the Free People, and they are the nearest thing the jungle has to the corporate life of civilized man. Shere Khan, as the lone tiger, represents disorder: a person loyal only to himself. He

Right:

UNNATURAL HISTORY:
A TIGER IN LONDON
ZOO. BEGINNING TO
LOOK TO THE FUTURE,
ZOOS ARE LINKING UP
WITH SCIENTIFIC
CAPTIVE-BREEDING
PROGRAMS.

Left:

BIG CAT ACTS WERE
ONCE A STANDARD
PART OF A CIRCUS.

lacks higher duties to a pack or to a civilization. But Kipling never tells unambiguous allegories, or makes unvarnished propaganda: over and over again, his storyteller's instincts override his imperial loyalties. And so the pack itself disintegrates and falls into anarchy, because it is not strong enough, with its noble but aging leader, to resist the will of Shere Khan.

Lord Baden-Powell used *The Jungle Book* as a bible for the younger members of the scouting movement, who are now called Cub Scouts, but originally they were Wolf Cubs. Baden-Powell, it seems, saw none of the thousand storyteller's ambiguities of Kipling's tales: he missed the subversive and anarchic streak that runs through the *Jungle Books* and saw only the imperial veneer of Kipling's mind. Mowgli, outcast, goes off to hunt alone: but his four wolf brothers go with him.

The western world occasionally had real tigers of its own, brought from Asia and placed in circuses and menageries. Naturally, the emphasis of the show was always on the tiger's ferocity, and therefore the extraordinary courage of the people who "tamed" them. Later, such wildlife freak shows acquired some measure of scientific respectability when they took the form of zoological gardens run by scientifically minded zoological societies. The mainstay of zoos has always been megafauna: lions and tigers, rhinoceros and elephants. Such animals have a long history as public diversions. These days, zoos are caught in a crisis of identity. They recognize that conservation is the priority, but many are unclear how best to achieve this in physical and organizational structures established in Victorian times.

The usefulness of zoos is always open to question. The traditional zoo inevitably tends to emphasize the gulf beween humans and animals: between gawper and gawpee. The traditional zoo celebrates not the animal but the cage. A project monitoring visitor behavior at the chimpanzee colony in Arnhem Zoo in the Netherlands recorded that the average visitor spent three and half minutes there; the most frequent remark was: "Oh, I could watch them for hours."

Tigers have always been a great exoticism, and another of the great tigers of literature makes his appearance as a weird and mistrusted outsider into a closed and cosy world. "Does Christopher Robin know about you?" asks Pooh, on meeting Tigger in A.A. Milne's *The House at Pooh Corner*. Tigger encounters a good deal of xenophobia in the forest, most

notably from Rabbit, who enlists Pooh and Piglet in a plot to moderate his behaviour: "Tigger's getting so bouncy nowadays that it's time we taught him a lesson." The lesson goes dreadfully wrong, and Tigger ends up rescuing Rabbit: "Oh Tigger, I am glad to see you."

A moral tale, but Tigger never really ceases to be an outsider. Tigger is isolated, except from his closest friend, the baby kangaroo called Roo, by his child-like nature. He is a foreigner, and a bit thick. He seems, in short, a nursery version of Kipling's notorious description of the savage: "half-devil and half-child." Tigger's first act at Pooh's house is to find a second Tigger, which happens to be in the mirror. His second is to attack the tablecloth, because it tried to bite him.

Below:

FEEDING TIME AT THE VICTORIAN ZOO: THE ZOO AS CELEBRATION, NOT OF THE ANIMAL'S STRENGTH BUT OF THE HUMAN POWER TO IMPRISON SUCH STRENGTH.

Left:

THE TIGER AS A
BEWILDERED AND
BEWILDERING OUT-
SIDER: TIGGER IS
NONPLUSED BY HIS
REFLECTION IN
*THE HOUSE AT POOH
CORNER.*

"I don't think it did," said Pooh.

"It tried," said Tigger. "But I was too quick for it."

But the Pooh stories, in which the locale is a child's mind, exhibit a basic (one might almost, if one wished to stretch a point, say a Hindu) tolerance, despite the widespread misgivings about Tigger. After Tigger had bounced, or perhaps coughed ("Well, I sort of boffed") Eeyore into the river, and Eeyore has been rescued, Pooh and Piglet talk over matters of the Forest with Christopher Robin, the child, or rather, since the Forest is his own mind, the Forest's ruling deity.

"Tigger is all right really," said Piglet lazily.

"Of course he is," said Christopher Robin.

"Everybody is really," said Pooh. "That's what I think," said Pooh. "But I don't suppose I'm right," he said.

"Of course you are," said Christopher Robin."

It is worth noting that even in the Pooh books, tigers are deeply ambiguous animals. You never know quite where you are with tigers.

Right

WILDERNESS. THIS IS
A VANISHING
COMMODITY IN AN
EVER-MORE CROWDED
WORLD.

EIGHT RACES

---

against

TIME

For thousands of years people worshipped tigers, made tigers symbols of courage and strength, wrote songs and poems to tigers, painted pictures of tigers, even dressed up as tigers and assumed tigrine virtues and power. And in all that period tigers flourished and people flourished; but people flourished more. That has changed everything, for people and for tigers. The balance has changed forever, people have gone on flourishing, and tigers - along with most of the rest of creation - have had to pay the price.

But until the seventeenth century, the tiger was a great success story: the niche of top predator was filled, as we have seen, in a fashion as close to perfection as nature is ever likely to get. The tiger was so versatile that it seemed that there were no circumstances it could not cope with. A couple of centuries ago - a mere eyeblink in terms of every form of history save that of human beings - the tiger was a creature in its evolutionary prime: vigorous, successful, at one with its complex variety of habitats.

Nothing has changed in evolutionary terms; but human beings have a knack that no other creature has ever managed. They are able to shift the goalposts of evolution, and to do so in a way that affects animals of other species than their

- our - own. The tiger is still in its prime, it takes more than a couple of centuries to change such a thing. But everything else is different, and the world's most fearsome hunter is now on the run. For the tiger species as a whole, the world has been changed from top to bottom.

The invention of firearms was the first major event in the tiger's decline. As early as the seventeenth century guns had become reasonably efficient machines for killing: they fired by a fairly reliable flintlock, and could fire a heavy bullet with considerable stopping power. With the development of accuracy and power came a reasonably safe method of killing what would otherwise be highly dangerous animals: that is what hunting means. Killing methods

Right:

THE DEVELOPMENT AND SPREAD OF EFFECTIVE FIREARMS CHANGED FOREVER THE BALANCE OF POWER BETWEEN TIGERS AND HUMANKIND.

Left:

THE TIGER HUNT AS
CELEBRATION: KING
GEORGE V DURING
THE KING EMPEROR'S
DURBAR TOUR OF
INDIA IN 1911. THE
KEEN OBSERVER WILL
NOTICE THAT THE
TIGERS HAVE LITTLE
CHANCE AGAINST THE
GUNS MASSED AGAINST
THEM FROM THE
GREAT HEIGHT OF AN
ELEPHANT'S BACK.

have got better and better: a modern rifle with a telescopic sight can kill a tiger 900 yards (900m) away. The automatic weapons of the military, with their colossal firepower, are still more effective devices, if slaughter is your aim.

Direct persecution was the first problem to affect tigers. It is a fact that direct persecution affects the top predator of an ecological system to a far greater extent than it does any animal further down the food chain. Prey species are far less vulnerable to the human hunter: after all, their society has been constructed on the premise that they will be hunted by one species or another. To generalize, there are always far more prey animals than predators: it is a truism of ecology that the population of prey animals dictates, to a large extent, the population of their predators. Systematic war against a predator will therefore have a drastic effect. In Britain, gamekeepers have deliberately shot or poisoned many birds which preyed, or even looked as if they might prey, on gamebirds - that is to say, birds protected to that the landowner might shoot them for "sport." This policy of extermination has caused local and national extinctions of birds of prey. A similar policy has had the same dramatic effect on populations of tigers.

The British led the way in tiger persecution with the craze - one might call it the mania - for tiger shooting. This was seen as a great and glorious pursuit: you proved your manhood by ridding the world of a demonic presence. It would be easier for the humans of the late twentieth century to claim the moral high ground

ATTAQUE PAR UN TIGRE

Above:

THERE WAS NEVER ANY DOUBT IN THE HUNTER'S MIND: KILLING TIGERS WAS A SERVICE TO HUMANITY. A FRENCH ILLUSTRATION DRAMATIZES THE TIGERS-AS-DEVILS PRINCIPLE.

above those of the nineteenth century if the there had been any slowing down in the loss of tigers; all that has changed is the the words and the reasons and the explanations. Major Walter Campbell wrote of one tiger: "A hellish fire shot from his eyes, and his whiskered lips curled into a grin of ineffable malignity as he gathered himself together for a decisive spring."

Tigers were devils, and it was right to

kill them. But as Victorian notions of fair play, sportsmanship and manliness developed, with sport and games a cornerstone of empire, hunters prided themselves increasingly on killing "in the right way." How a tiger was killed became increasingly important: certainly it overrode any question of why. The tiger was to be shot cleanly: wounded animals must not be left to a lingering death. But most tigers were shot from comparative safety: from an elephant's back, or from the top of a tree. The tiger was generally attracted to a tethered bait, or driven towards the guns by beaters.

The tiger acquired the cachet of the hunter's ultimate quarry. In Africa, in many places you can see across the plains for miles and lion hunting, even on foot, can be made comparatively straightforward. In the thick cover of tiger country, more could go wrong, the hunter was in more danger - and the tiger became more and more desirable.

If bagging a tiger was a good thing, multiple bags were obviously better. Serious "sportsmen" wanted to score their century of tigers, and many managed to do so. But the most ardent Victorian sportsmen who arrived in India were outdone by Indian royalty. More British than the British, they naturally had to shoot even more tigers. The champion of them all was the Maharajah of Surguja, whose lifetime total was 1,150 tigers. He was eventually declared insane by the British government - though not for killing tigers - was removed from power and died in 1950. Even after the mad tiger killer was

Left:

TIGERS GREW
INCREASINGLY WARY
UNDER THE PRESSURE
OF CEASELESS HUNT-
ING. FROM THEIR
UNWILLINGNESS TO
STAND UP AND BE
KILLED GREW THE
MYTH OF THE COW-
ARDLY TIGER.

STATUS OF TIGER POPULATION 1994

TIGER SUBSPECIES	MINIMUM	MAXIMUM	AUTHORITY
BENGAL (INDIAN) TIGER *P.t. tigris* (Linnaeus 1758)	3,250	4,700	
Bangladesh	300	460	Khan/Coudhury, Forest Dept 1994
Bhutan	50	240	Forest Dept/WWF Report 1993 Dorji 1994
India	2,750	3,750	Project Tiger/Indian experts 1994
Nepal	150	250	Wildlife Dept/IUCN Report 1993
CASPIAN (HYRCANIAN/TURAN) TIGER *P.t. virgata* (Illiger 1815) Formerly Afghanistan, Iran, Chinese and Russian Turkestan, Turkey	extinct 1970s		
SIBERIAN (AMUR/USSURI/NORTH-EAST CHINA/ MACHURIAN) TIGER *P.t. altaica* (Temminck 1844)	150	200	
China	present		Tan 1992
Korea (North)	<10	<10	Pak U Il 1994
Russia	150	200	Amirkhanov 1994
JAVAN TIGER *P.t. sondaica* (Temminck 1844):	?extinct 1980s		Tiger sign report being checked 1993
SOUTH CHINA (AMOY) TIGER *P.t. amoyensis* (Hilzheimer 1905): China	30	80	Tan/Lu/Shen 1986
BALI TIGER *P.t. balica* (Schwarz 1912)	extinct 1940s		
SUMATRAN TIGER *P.t. sumatrae* (Pocock 1929)	600	650	Tilson 1993
INDOCHINESE TIGER *P.t. corbetti* (Mzak 1968)	1,050	1,750	
Cambodia	100	200	Chhim Somean 1994
Laos	present		Salter 1993
Malaysia	600	650	Elugapillai 1994
Myanmar (formerly Burma)	present		Forest Dept 1993
Thailand	150	600	Rabinowitz 1993 Schwann 1994
Vietnam	200	300	Nguyen 1994
TOTALS	5,080	7,380	
ROUNDED TOTALS	5,000	7,400	

Note: Estimates for *P.t. Corbetti* in Myanmar also include *P.t. tigris*. Estimates for 1993 are combined with those given at the Global Tiger Forum (GTF), New Delhi, 1994.

Table compiled by Peter Jackson, Chairman, Cat Specialist Group, Species Survival Commission, The World Conservation Union (IUCN).

deposed, his regency government took over where he left off. Sane or mad, ruling Rajah or regent, it was all one to the tigers.

Tiger hunting lived on and lived on. As recently as 1961, Queen Elizabeth II of England and her husband Prince Philip made a tour of of India, and visited Rantahambore, which is now a nature reserve. The prince took part in a tiger shoot, and the party managed to kill tigers - two of them, in fact.

As hunters continued on their self-applauding way, they affected the behavior of the tigers. From this came the myth of the tiger as coward. As hunting increased and spread - one hunter wrote that "every tiger in India has been hunted" - tigers got better and better at keeping out of hunters' way. They avoided, as far as possible, all contact with people. They became harder and harder to find and to kill. They avoided humans, which was hardly surprising when most humans they encountered were seeking to blow them to bits, but this eminently sensible behavior was seen as cowardice. Tigers, it seemed, didn't know about fair play. Their behavior at kills changed. Many would never go back

Above:

THE MAN OF EMPIRE IN APOTHEOSIS: A HUNTER POSES OVER A DEAD TIGER.

Opposite:

THE TIGER IS SELDOM SEEN IN FULL DAYLIGHT; BUT NATURALISTS HAVE SPECULATED THAT TIGERS HAVE SWITCHED FROM DAYTIME TO NIGHT-TIME ANIMALS IN ORDER TO AVOID HUMAN HUNTERS.

to a kill once a meal had been taken from it. Hunters who waited for hours by the remains, their rifles at the ready, were increasingly waiting in vain. The tiger was rejecting its execution; therefore the tiger was a coward.

The fact is that the tiger was getting wise to hunters. Some observers have even said that the nocturnal life of the tiger developed as a survival strategy. Nocturnal living is not, perhaps, a tigrine tradition from the birth of the species, but a recently developed improvisation that allowed them to avoid contact with hunters. Tigers learned to lie up during the day in order to avoid discovery and the merciless guns. They learned to hunt under cover of night, to avoid being hunted. Several observers, most particularly Fateh Singh Rathore of Ranthambhore, have found that tigers, when assured of a safe, gunfree environment, are happy to have their being in the daylight.

It is easy to see how the death of a single tiger can destabilize a tiger population. The death of a territorial male tiger creates a vacancy in what was once his territory. The vacancy will, given a healthy tiger population, be taken up pretty promptly; though not necessarily without bloodshed, and perhaps a further death or two. And once the new tiger has taken over, he is likely to seek out all the tigresses whose territories fall within his own super-territory. If he finds them with cubs, he is likely to kill the cubs. The female will then bear his own thus one bullet can put back the tiger civilization of that region up to two years.

And it doesn't stop there. Hunting and persecution do not end with a single shot. The new territorial male, big and fierce and clearly desirable as a trophy, is likely to become a target himself. He might well get shot within two years, before his cubs have left their various mothers. So he is killed and once again there is a vacancy. The situation repeats itself: and once again, further deaths of adults and cubs are likely to follow, and still no new young adults have been recruited to the population. If you keep killing big males, it becomes impossible to raise cubs. The constant replacement of the top male can lead to constant infanticide.

As time moved on, a second problem was added: that of competition for space with human beings. Such competition, once set in motion, is always won by humans. The tigers have been hammered on every side, and the pace of their destruction has shown an alarming propensity to speed up.

It is clear, then, that there are plenty of grim facts about tigers which must not be ducked. The examination of what has gone wrong for tigers is the first step towards putting things right. It must be stressed, even as we begin to examine the problems that tigers have faced, still face, and will continue to face, that there is a good deal of will to solve them. The tiger is no hopeless case. But if we want to save the tiger we must look at the problems squarely, before moving on to their solution. No cause, and certainly not that of the tiger, is well served by depression and despair.

All the same, it must be admitted that

it does not make happy reading. At the beginning of the twentieth century it is reckoned that there were probably 100,000 tigers left in the wild. Today, estimates put the total population at somewhere between 5,300 and 7,400, as the table shows.

The Indian tiger is doing best. Numbers are reckoned at betwen 3,000 and 5,000. Most of these are in India itself, with a few hundred in Nepal and Bangladesh, and perhaps 50 in Bhutan. Some Indian figures represent an actual rise in population. These figures, however, have produced disbelief and dismay: we shall look at this conundrum later. There are twelve regions of India which have significant tiger populations, the biggest of these areas being the Sunderbans, which extends east into Bangladesh. The Nepalese tigers are scattered over three centres of population. There are also some Indian tigers in the west of Burma.

The IndoChinese tiger has populations in Cambodia, Laos, Vietnam, Thailand, Myanmar (formerly Burma) and Malaysia. Accurate estimates of numbers are even more difficult to obtain than usual: with some populations, the best information available is that tigers are "present". Numbers between 800 and 2,000 have been postulated. The thing is that no one actually knows. Perhaps only the Thai figure of 600 can be considered accurate but even this has been challenged as some conservationists believe that the figure may be as low as 150. The Malaysian population is interesting, insofar as the evidence

suggests that there is very little poaching in that country although it would take a brave person to rule out the possibility completely. Tiger poaching is a global problem, but Malaysia has remained immune thanks to good protection of national parks. However, the Malaysians have destroyed a great deal of tiger habitat: their enthusiastic plundering of their own rainforests has been devastating. This race has further problems in that three of the states in its range are not signatories to CITES, the Convention on International Trade in Endangered Species, these being Laos, Cambodia, and Myanmar. However, Myanmar and Cambodia are to apply shortly.

The Sumatran tiger comes next, with populations estimated at 400. They are found in five different areas, with no chance of movement between them. This highlights a conservation problem with many species of mammal: lack of mobility. Isolated populations exist on an ever smaller gene pool: the stock thus loses the vigor brought by constant infusions of new blood. Wild pig is the staple prey item of the Sumatran tiger, through they also take good numbers of sambar deer and monkeys.

After that, the Siberian tiger population is said to be around 250, perhaps as many as 400. Siberian tigers are found in the Primoskye and Khabarovsk regions. These areas are inhospitable not only to men but to most forms of life; Siberia is no place of tropical abundance. Prey populations are widely spread: tigers must adopt a similar pattern of life. The territories of Siberian tigers are consequently vast. Wild pig is their commonest prey species. The Siberian tiger extends into nothern China. At one stage, the Siberians went as far as Korea, but the tiger has almost gone now from North Korea and has completely gone from South Korea.

There are still a few Chinese tigers left in the wild, very few: fewer than 50 animals. The population is very close to being nonviable: beyond saving. The Chinese tiger has been brought to this pass by a political pogrom. The Chinese government established a huge program to maximize land for agriculture during the 1960s and 1970s. The tiger was regarded as a pest species, inappropriate to modern China, and was deliberately and systematically wiped out.

The 50-odd surviving Chinese tigers are widely scattered, and it seems unlikely that they still have viable breeding populations. There are wild tiger in four provinces, in Hunan, Juiangsi, Fujian and Guangdong. This is a sad decline from a population that was around 3,000 just a couple of decades back.

The Chinese tiger is, if evolutionary speculation is correct, the species from which all other tigrine races diverged: the direct descendant of the ancestral *Felis paleosinesis*. The Chinese tiger is on the point, it seems, of following its ancestor into extinction. Here there is no escape from human guilt. The Chinese government declared the tiger a pest, as if it were a large stripey rat. It was "harmful to agricultural and pastoral progress," so it was persecuted and shot until it now stands on the cusp of extinction.

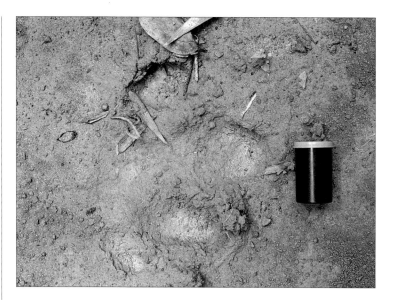

The Chinese policy of the deliberate destruction of the tiger was not the first of its kind. The Soviets actually sent the army in ahead of farmers to exterminate the Caspian tiger, and it must be said that they did a fine job. The Caspian forests and the reedbeds of the Caspian sea were cleared: the Caspian tiger has gone, and so has its habitat. Thus passes one of the great biological systems of the world. It was a great, an absolutely massive crime against conservation. Condemning the atrocity is easy, but one must beware of the dangers of getting self-congratulatory on behalf of the West. The West has committed just as many crimes, amd just as spectacular, starting with its financial involvement in the destruction of tropical forests all over the world.

The Caspian tiger was last seen in 1967. Some fresh skins were found in the range area in 1972, but it is not certain that these were the skins of local tigers. And certainly there has been no sign of a

Above:

TIGER PUGMARK: READING THESE ENIGMATIC TRACES OF TIGER PASSAGE IS AN ESSENTIAL SKILL IN THE COUNTING OF TIGER POPULATIONS.

Above:

TASTEFUL SOUVENIRS:
A GIFT-SHOP IN
SINGAPORE DEMON-
STRATES SOME OF THE
101 USES FOR A DEAD
TIGER.

Caspian tiger since. That race has certainly been lost.

The Javan tiger has not been seen since the early 1980s, at which time there were said to be five individuals left. There have been occasional reports of sightings since, and occasional discoveries of tracks, scratch marks, and even findings of tiger hair. A two-year search project operated by the World Wide Fund for Nature (WWF) ended in 1994. This used up-to-date techniques such as photo trapping, which have been startlingly effective in locating other scarce animals such as the Javan rhinoceros. But two years of search turned up not a single tiger: it is possible that the reported sightings and signs were of leopard rather than tiger. In Java, one of the most densely populated areas of the world, the tiger had for some years been living on borrowed time: now it is surely gone. If, perhaps, one or two tigers exist and have avoided the searchers, then they are unlikely to be enough to maintain a stable breeding population. If there are any left at all, the population has certainly dipped below viability.

And the Bali tiger is long gone. The last known Bali tiger was shot in 1937. By the beginning of the Second World War it was certainly extinct. There are occasional reports of tiger sightings, but since Bali is an an island of Hinduism and magic, it is considered that these were sightings of spirit tigers - intriguing enough particularly to the anthropologist, but not strictly relevant to the naturalist. Bali is a small island and very heavily cultivated: there is no tiger habitat left.

To sum up: the tiger diversified into eight races. There are only five of them left. One is in imminent danger of extinction, two more in extreme peril, and two more are hanging on in the face of mounting problems.

But there is also a major problem with all these figures quoted above. They are at best approximate. The fact is that it is extremely hard to take an accurate census of tigers. They are simply not amenable beasts: secretive, loving darkness and cover, and often prefering rugged and - to humans - inhospitable terrain. Much census work has been done by tracking, a method that depends on the ability of the tracker to identify individual tigers from their "pugmarks" - the technical term for footprints. Figures from such methods depend heavily on the skill of the tracker, and it is a method that has been much criticized.

Tiger figures, like every other kind of figures ever collated, are subject to manipulation, and adjustment upwards

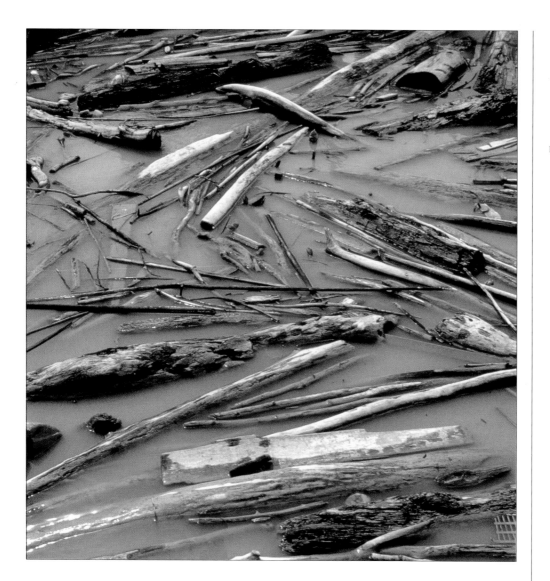

Left:

HABITAT DESTRUC-
TION: THE LOGGING
INDUSTRY HAS
CHANGED THE FACE
OF ASIA. IT HAS
DESTROYED COMPLEX
ECOSYSTEMS, AND HAS
DESTROYED TIGER
POPULATIONS.

or downwards, on Mark Twain's "lies, damned lies,and statistics" principle. It is suspected that, for complex political reasons, there has been a good deal of fudging of tiger statistics. If your job depends on optimistic tiger figures, by a strange coincidence you tend to come up with good tiger figures. The political tiger is a beast we shall look at in later chapters; meanwhile, it is enough to understand that all these bald tigrine facts of population are not altogether reliable.

Other census methods are also open to doubt. A simple sum involving the known tiger density and the area of tiger habitat is useful enough as a computation, but it is never more than an approximation. Of necessity, it cannot take in local factors. It is a broad generalization, and like all generalizations (including this one) it is inaccurate.

Most figures reveal a decline in tiger numbers. But many Indian figures represent an increase: if swallowed whole, it would seem that the rise in tiger numbers here has provided a perfect counterweight to the decline elsewhere in the world. You could even twist them enough to demonstrate that the world tiger population was pretty well stable. However, the tigers would tell a different story. Various non-official estimates of tiger numbers shatter such hopes. Some say that the estimates of the Indian tiger population have been so wildly exaggerated that there is less than half the number of tigers officially claimed. If the unofficial figures represent anything like the real facts, they would demonstrate what is accepted by conservationists across the world: that here too tigers are facing a familiar scenario of catastrophe.

Catastrophe began, but only began, with the hunt. The direct persecution of the tiger had an increasingly drastic effect on numbers all over the world, whether this was done for "sport" or as part of a government sponsored program of "pest control." The development of the four-wheel drive off-road vehicle made vast tracts of tiger habitat of easy access to men with guns.

The tiger received a further blow with the broadening of the base of persecution - what might be called the democratization of tiger slaying. Certainly, traditional Asian communities had in some places caught tigers in fall traps, or used poisoned carcasses to kill them. This was normally for self-protection. It was not until the Second World War that firearms became widely available throughout Asia. Other crises brought still more human catastrophe and therefore guns from one end of the continent to the other. The partition of India and the subsequent disputes inevitably brought huge quantities of firearms in their wake.

And so, in the postwar years, the nature of tiger shooting changed. It became less and less the exclusive pastime of the rich and the royal, more and more a commercial activity. Self-protection was still sometimes the reason for the slaying of a tiger, but it was far more often the excuse. Tiger skins were worth money. Anyone with a gun could make serious money by shooting tigers and selling the skins. Tiger skins ended up in the West. They were used as exotic ornaments or garments. Increasing scarcity only raised demand.

As it became clear that tiger numbers were declining with uncontrolable rapidity, the realization affected hunting people. Some of them gave up hunting entirely: many of the great early heroes of conservation are reformed hunters. But sad to say, these outbreaks of sanity were not visited on every hunter. The increasing scarcity of the tiger only inspired many to seek one. They wanted to bag their tiger before the tigers had all gone. Americans, Japanese, Germans, and the oil-rich princes of the Middle East converged on India to shoot their tiger before it was too late. The first inklings of the tiger's possible extinction gave a huge spur to its persecutors. Meanwhile demand for tiger skins soared, and so did the prices. India

banned trade in tiger skins, but that only pushed the business underground.

And even where there were no firearms, agricultural poisons, ever more easily available, were used to kill tigers for money. Poisoned carcasses killed and still kill many other creatures with a taste for scavenging, jackals and vultures in particular. Throughout their range, tigers were the target of direct persecution. All this was certainly enough to push the tiger towards extinction. But as the twentieth century rolled on, a still greater problem emerged.

You don't have to kill tigers to kill tigers. Kill the jungle and the tigers will die. The destruction of tigers has been bad enough, but the destruction of tiger habitat is simply devastating. Take Ranthambhore, which is, as we have seen, one of the great tiger reserves of the world. It has become an island, surrounded by land that has been grazed to near destruction. In drought years, this becomes virtual desert. Legal and physical protection has kept Ranthambhore safe from the terrible manmade process of desertification; but that only makes the lush grasses within its boundaries more tempting. Graziers have turned

their cattle into the tiger reserve in tens of thousands.

Another example is that of another Indian reserve, Nagarahole. The reserve contains 50 tigers in 250 sq miles (650sq km). On the borders of the reserve stand 250 villages. The Indian population has grown by 300 million since the early 1970s. They have felled trees, cultivated wild places, grazed their cattle, and cleared land to find living space.

The human species needs more and more space to live, to grow crops, to graze livestock. The population of Asia continues to soar. More land is needed. More and more land is taken up, often for the merest short-term gain. With every clearance a patch of jungle is gone forever. Often, land so avidly seized becomes good for neither man nor beast: it can be grazed only for a few seasons before it becomes over-grazed to the point of desertification. And so the cycle continues, and the graziers seek new land for their beasts.

Technology has brought insecticides which can wipe out malarial mosquitoes that once made vast areas of tiger-habitat quite impossible for humans. As people moved into these areas, this tiger habitat too was destroyed.

Logging has added an additional pressure onto the tigers of the Asian rainforest. The destruction of the tropical forest has been chronicled many times, and need not be repeated here. But global anguish about the fall of the forests has done little to slow the devastating speed of their destruction.

At the heart of this destruction lies one of history's great errors of understanding. Tropical forests are unbelievably lush and fertile: therefore, the false reasoning goes, the land they grow must be wonderfully fertile, and must surely yield wonderfully lush crops. Not so: a rainforest is its own closed system. The rainforest is self-sufficient, fed and nourished by itself. The soil on which it stands is shallow and fragile. The destruction of rainforest creates not sumptuous farmland but mile after mile of near desert. Southeast Asia has lost half its forest. Only 14 percent of Indian forests remain: 24 percent of Thailand's forests, 9.3 percent of Bangladesh's. Malaysia managed to get rid of 41.5 percent of its forests in a decade.

Increasingly, then, there is a pattern of besieged tiger reserves surrounded by open country. There is less and less peripheral habitat: fewer and fewer of the viable, but sub-optimal ideal places where tigers used to be found on the limits of their ranges. That means that there are fewer and fewer places for wandering, territoryless tigers: in particular, there are fewer places for the young males. These bold and dashing wanderers are, as it were, the team reserves, the stand-ins waiting for the chance to make their breakthrough and to join the first team of breeding males. But increasingly they have nowhere to go while they wait, nowhere to hide, nowhere to hunt and nowhere in which to wander. There is a terrible shortage of "wildlife corridors," the wild areas that link one area of prime jungle with another.

Young male tigers are roamers, and are

Opposite:

CULTURAL SCHIZO-
PHRENIA: METROZOO
IN FLORIDA PARADES
ITS TIGERS BEFORE A
REPLICA OF THE 13TH
CENTURY SHRINE OF
ANGKOR WAT.

accustomed to try their luck over a wide range of country. They have little to lose, they will explore, learn and improvise: they will take risks in hunting that few fully adult tigers will consider. It is, as we have seen, a tough life, and not all these wanderers are smart enough, strong enough or lucky enough to make it into the breeding population.

But as they wander, often miles from the places where they were born, the best and the luckiest eventually become breeding tigers. The young males, then, are not idlers and wastrels: nor are they a side issue. They are the future. For often, in the natural way of things, they would eventually get lucky and take over a territory remote from their native jungle. Thus they would bring fresh blood into the population. In this way populations of tigers are constantly reinvigorated. But this absolutely essential process of reinvigoration happens less and less. Small isolated populations cut off from other communities become weakened, subject more and more to inbreeding and hereditary weakness. A shallow gene pool gives a population no resilience. A shallow gene pool makes a population vulnerable.

Yet more problems to tiger habitat were caused by war. War in Korea and Vietnam devastated the forests of those countries. Napalm, bombs and shells have wrecked vast areas of jungle. Furthermore, forests were quite deliberately ruined as an act of war. Huge areas of Vietnamese forests were notoriously treated with defoliant, an arsenic-based poison. The destruction of the forests was one of the most efficient operations that the United States were able to perform in the war. Defoliants make an extremely effective weapon - if destroying tigers is your aim.

Tigers still hang on in Vietnam, and were able, on occasions, to turn war to their profit. More than once they were seen scavenging the corpses of soldiers, and there are occasional records of tigers attacking troops. But war, disruption, and destruction bring only occasional bonuses: the long-term effects have been severely destructive.

The tiger, then, has suffered on two fronts. The first is direct persecution: a deliberate war on the tiger for "sport," for self-protection, and for money. The second is inadvertant. War: agriculture, dwellings. Many people who live close to tigers may well have the most benign feelings towards them. Nevertheless, their priority will be the feeding of themselves and their families. In the recent past the tiger has suffered from mischief and profiteering. But now, it seems. we have discovered the greatest enemy of all: the ordinary decent person trying to make a living.

The tiger has been succcesfully bred in captivity many times, but it is hard to see what good this does. True, the worldwide zoo population of tiger numbers can be maintained without depleting the wild stock, but that is a fairly limited objective. The problem is that the chances of a captive-bred tiger's survival in the wild are almost non-existent. Zoos cannot duplicate the long education a mother can give her cubs: without it, a tiger cannot survive. There have been some intriguing experiements carried out at Madhav National Park in India, where tigers in a large enclosure were introduced to free running animals. They killed these on a number of occasions; but there is a difference between knocking over a domestic chicken and ambushing a fully grown deer.

Besides, the main conservation problem in the world is not declining numbers, but habitat loss. There is no point in releasing tigers into the wild if there is no wild left. The argument that captive animals stand as totems - as, if you like, the public relations men for their species - is not convincing. In fact, many people in zoos consider the "megafauna" approach to zookeeping out of date, inappropriate to the times. Such people are considering, and some are actually going ahead with, plans to end their dealings with big cats.

A modern zoo prides itself on being a conservational and educational organization. But, it must bring paying customers through the gate, or it cannot survive financially. Zoos must balance the pointlessness of keeping, say, a tiger in captivity with the need for a big, dramatic animal as an attraction. But increasingly, many zoos are wrestling with that conundrum. To keep an animal solely to draw in visitors seems less and less acceptable. Zoos are seeking a wider cultural and scientific role, in which the captive tiger will perhaps have a lesser part to play.

The tiger is beset by problems and complications. At the end, it seems to come down to a simple choice between people or tigers; between short-term benefits for farmers and long-term survival for tigers. But such a choice is simply impossible. Instead, the far more difficult middle way must be found: the mutual understanding of farmers and conservationsists, the integration of people and tigers. It is one of the many absolutely colossal challenges of global conservation. Traditional communities lived alongside tigers and established a relationship of respect, admiration, and deference to the great beasts. In new times, a new way must be found for reestablishing an ancient understanding and tolerance.

Right

THE WORLD WOKE UP
TO THE PROSPECT OF
ECODISASTER A
TERRIFYINGLY SHORT
TIME AGO. GREAT
BEASTS AND GREAT
OPEN SPACES: FOR
HOW MUCH LONGER
WILL WE HAVE THEM?

The
GREAT
AWAKENING

SOMETHING ODD HAPPENED TO THE WORLD IN THE LATE 1960S
AND EARLY 1970S. IT WAS AS IF THE HUMAN RACE WOKE UP FROM
A PROFOUND SLUMBER, AND BEGAN TO LURCH, EYE-RUBBING,
SLEEPY AND STILL ONLY HALF-CONSCIOUS, INTO THE WAKING
WORLD. THE GAP BETWEEN DREAMS AND THE REAL WORLD IS
ALWAYS COLOSSAL: ALWAYS HARD TO SPAN.

THROUGHOUT HISTORY HUMANS HAD LIVED IN A DREAM
OF PLENTY. NATURE SEEMED BOUNDLESS AND PERPETUALLY SELF-
RENEWING. HUMANS, PART BENEFICIARIES OF KINDLY MOTHER
NATURE, PART ADVERSARIES OF NATURE RED IN TOOTH AND CLAW,
HAD NEVER SEEN THE NATURAL WORLD AS ANYTHING OTHER THAN
A BOTTOMLESS WELL. NATURE, WILDLIFE - PLENTY-MORE-WHERE-
THAT-CAME-FROM.

Right:

FOR MANY YEARS THE SLAUGHTER OF TIGERS WAS A WAY OF LIFE. HERE TIGER SKINS ARE PROUDLY DISPLAYED. ANYONE WHO RAISED ANY OBJECTIONS WAS WRITTEN OFF AS A CRANK.

This belief was maintained in the face of a series of dreadful warnings. In the previous century the American bison, sometimes called buffalo, the dominant herbivore of a continent, had been brought to virtual extinction, partly because of the traditional plenty-more-where-that-came-from thinking, and partly as a deliberate attempt to destroy the way of life of the indigenous people of North America. War against the buffalo was war against the Indians; the Indians and the buffalo lost.

Perhaps one could claim that this slaughter was exceptional, based as it was on political expedient. But it is hard to find a reason for the extinction of the passenger pigeon. This seems to have been be a matter of simple carelessness. The passenger pigeon was one of the most numerous, if not the most numerous species of bird ever to live. The only possible rival is the quelea of Africa. People saw flocks of passenger pigeons 4 miles (6km) long and 1 mile (1.6km) broad, million upon million of passenger pigeons, flocks that blackened the sky. Nesting colonies covered 30sq miles (12sq km); strings of colonies stretched 100 miles (160km) in length. And they were shot in equally colossal numbers. One hunting competition did not award a prize to anyone with a bag of less than 30,000 birds. The last passenger pigeon died in Cincinnati Zoo on September 1, 1914. Humans had wiped out what was the commonest bird in the world: perhaps the commonest bird in the history of the world. Nothing, surely, was now beyond the human talent for slaughter.

It took rather more than 50 years from the death of the last passenger pigeon -

her name was Martha, by the way - before humans began to come to terms with their - our - power for destruction. Conservation organizations had existed for some time, but largely as marginalized groups. Conservation was seen as the domain of cranks and sentimentalists. "The trouble is these sort of people get really worked up about their damned birds or whatever it is ... So I'm supposed to do what? Send a submarine off to the island? For what? To find out what's happened to a covey of pink storks." These are the words of James Bond's boss, M, in *Dr No*, first published in 1958; words that reflected the general feelings of power brokers in the early 1960s, and a line of thinking far from extinct today.

But the point is that, as the 1960s progressed, it became increasingly clear that the cranks and sentimentalists were right; the hard-headed, clear-sighted people of affairs were wrong. M, seeing only politics and international crookery, was wrong: crisis was at hand. (And as a matter of fact, *Dr No* is full of the author Ian Fleming's own love of the natural world, expressed in the character of Honeychile Rider, but that is by the by.)

As the decade marched on, the looming extinction of large mammals began to attract global concern: the white rhino, the panda, the blue whale. The notion of extinction at last began to seize the world's imagination. At last the inflexible thinking of centuries had been broken.

Left:

VERY GRADUALLY, THINGS BEGAN TO CHANGE FOR THE TIGER. THESE ORNAMENTAL TIGER SKINS WERE CONFISCATED IN BANGKOK EN ROUTE FROM DELHI. NOTE THE ARTIFICIALLY CREATED "FEROCITY" OF EXPRESSION.

Opposite:

THE TIDE TURNED AS
A NETWORK OF
RESERVES WAS ESTAB-
LISHED. PERIYAR
TIGER RESERVE WAS
SET UP IN KERALA,
SOUTHERN INDIA.

The sensible householder calls the plumber in when there is a leak. In this case no one thought of calling the plumber until the flood was lapping at the attic.

The tiger was not, at first, seen as an animal in crisis. It was still cheerfully hunted throughout the 1960s; as we have seen, Prince Philip himself was involved in a tiger shoot. The first significant date in tiger conservation was 1969. Endangered animals are listed in what are known as Red Data books produced by the International Union for Conservation of Nature and Natural Resources (IUCN). These documents state the "official" line on which species are in danger and which are not. On the basis of these Red Data books, strategies and priorities for conservation can be worked out.

Seven of the tiger subspecies had been entered in the Red Data Book, but the Indian tiger was considered safe; therefore the species as a whole was not regarded as endangered. Kailash Sankhala changed all that. Sankhala, Director of Delhi Zoo, made a two-year study of tiger numbers, while the Bombay Natural History Society carried out a survey by questionnaire. Both initiatives reached the same conclusion: tiger numbers were down to 2,500 and declining fast. In 1969 the IUCN admitted the Indian tiger to the world's list of endangered animals. This gave the tiger full protection as a species. The tiger was at last officially "endangered". With every passing year, this is less exclusive.

The short history of conservation, a tale of occasional heroic achievements and the dull thudding of regular, terrifying reverses, is concerned with the business of political will. Conservationists need to persuade politicians, first that something needs to be done, and second, that they must actually go ahead and do it. Neither is easy; of the two the second is probably the harder.

A general assembly of the IUCN was held in 1969 in New Delhi, which was a useful starting point for influencing the hearts and minds of Indian politicians. When politicians are reluctant to move, they stall by insisting on more evidence, more hard facts, more research: no question of a move without trebly certain proofs. It has always been the case that conservationists must prove every case up to the hilt, while other lobbies, representing commercial and other interests more close to normal political priorities, have been able to force decisions on scanty evidence. It is hard to gather accurate figures on any kind of wildlife and, as we know, the tiger specializes in elusiveness. As far as many Indian politicians were concerned, the tiger was a common, inevitable part of India, and always would be.

Yet the tiger dominated that session of IUCN in 1969, and the passion of Sankhala and other Indian conservationists had a great deal to do with this. The assembly called for all tiger range states to ban the hunting of tigers and the export of their skins. Also, to face the politicians with the facts, an all-India tiger census was decided on, with Sankhala in charge.

It was then that Guy Mountfort, a British conservationist and a founder

Right:

A DREAM REALIZED: A
WELL-FED MOTHER
WITH HER CUBS IN
BANDHAVGHAR
NATIONAL PARK IN
INDIA.

trustee of WWF (then the World Wildlife Fund, now the Worldwide Fund for Nature), decided that this organization should raise a million American dollars to launch Operation Tiger. He started collecting donations on a flight to Florida with the WWF president, Prince Bernhard of the Netherlands. He launched a number of special events in America for this project, for which he had yet to receive formal WWF backing.

Mountfort's next idea was to fly to Delhi and harangue Indira Gandhi, then Prime Minister of India, moving on to excite pro-tiger sympathies in the governments of Nepal and Bangladesh. A joint meeting of the IUCN and WWF was skeptical of his chances of success. But Mountfort got their support, aided by Charles de Haes, then an aide to Prince Bernhard and later WWF Director General.

The meeting with Indira Gandhi was perhaps the turning of the tide. In fact, one individual took it upon herself to turn the tide personally. Where Canute failed, Indira Gandhi succeeded. Mountfort spelt out the tiger's acute peril and offered a solution: dedicated tiger reserves, scientifically managed, properly researched. This was the way the world's tigers would be saved, and WWF was raising a million dollars to make it happen.

Mrs Gandhi was on his side in an instant. "I shall form a special committee. A Tiger Task Force. And it will report to me personally." It was the best news the tiger had had in decades.

One slight embarrassment was that Mrs Gandhi assumed that the million dollars was all for India, and no one dared to tell her otherwise. So WWF found a further $800,000, to go to Nepal, Indonesia and Thailand.

At this stage serious attempts to assess the world population of tigers were made. Occasionally, in any walk of life, a number will turn up: a figure so vivid that it seems to tell the entire story: a statistic that dramatizes and brings into focus all the essential points of a certain situation. Call this the "killer-stat". The tiger population of India - India, a country thought to be seething with tigers, the tiger country, a country where, so far as tigers were

concerned, there were now and always had been plenty-more-where-that-came-from – was now just 1,827. This was the figure that, it can be said, changed the course of tiger history – the killer-stat.

Opposite:

GREEN TOURISM: A PARTY WATCHES A TIGER FROM THE BACK OF AN ELEPHANT. CONTROLLED TOURISM PLACES A DOLLAR VALUE ON CONSERVATION.

Compare and contrast with an estimated global population of 100,000 at the turn of the century. Researchers also made estimates for the tiger populations of neighboring countries, necessarily approximate. They produced a figure for the entire global population of the Indian race of the tiger, *Panthera tigris tigris*. They reckoned it at 2,400.

The killer-stat: a figure that brought the end of complacency, the end of the plenty-more-where-that-came-from attitude. The figure spelt out the truly desperate state of the Indian tiger; and the fact that India bore the greatest responsibility if the beast was to be saved.

Research broadened to the other races of tiger: by the end of the 1960s it was generally accepted that three of the eight races of tiger were extinct, or were about to become extinct. This, as we know, is what happened: as the 1970s began, it was clear for the first time that the Bali, the Caspian and the Javan tigers were all either going or gone. And gone they certainly are now. Nor did it end there: it seemed clear, even back in the early 1970s, that the Chinese tiger was likely to be the next one to go. Thus the dominant carnivore of Asia, a beast whose range had covered most of the continent, was now surviving in pockets, hemmed in by the march of destruction and the ever increasing demands of an ever increasing human population. Any figure for a world population would involve a number of guesses, but the most optimistic estimate was that 7,000 or 8,000 tigers remained in the world's wild places.

The tiger had two things on its side: two things to demand the attention. The first is - to use an outmoded public relations term - that the tiger is one of the world's sexiest animals. It commands massive public appeal: the name and the image of tiger have, as we have seen, deep echoes in the culture of both East and West; and the living tiger probably impresses people more than any other animal on earth. Secondly, there is the notion of extinction. Nothing commands the attention like extinction: it is, if you like, the sexiest concept in conservation. The shocking truth that the tiger was on the verge of extinction brought a powerful emotional reaction all over the world. The tiger: extinction: it was a double-fisted assault on the world's consciousness.

And so it all began. A series of conservation projects followed: Project Tiger, Operation Tiger, and so on. Every one of them has a wonderful name: names that gain their force, in emotional and political terms, because just about any phrase containing the word "tiger" cannot help but have a huge impact. Operation Tiger was officially launched in September 1972; both the tiger's troubles, and the enormous efforts that were now being made to end them, captured the world's attention.

Enthusiasm spread, partly because of Indira Gandhi's efforts, partly because the push by conservationists continued. Bangladesh and Nepal also committed themselves to the conservation of the tiger and to the establishing of projects for the preservation of its habitat. Such

Right:

A MOTHER AND HER
MALE CUB: IMAGES
LIKE THIS MADE CON-
SERVATIONISTS
REJOICE AS THE NET-
WORK OF TIGER
RESERVES SPREAD
ACROSS ASIA.
CONSERVATIONISTS
BELIEVED THAT THEY
HAD SUCCEEDED IN
SAVING THE TIGER.
BUT THEIR CELEBRA-
TIONS WERE PREMA-
TURE.

projects were good news for tigers, and also good news for all wilderness-dwelling beasts. If you wish to save the sexy animal at the top of the food chain, you must save its habitat. If you do that, you cannot help but save all the other creatures that live in the habitat: species after species, large mammals, birds, ants, the lot. Though the term "biodiversity" was not coined for another 20 years, Operation Tiger and its sister projects all struck powerful blows for preservation of life's endless varieties.

The IUCN and WWF agreed that the tiger was now a leading priority. Their principal strategy was the creation of tiger reserves: the conservation of tigrine habitat. It sounds simple enough, but in truth it is an endlessly complicated business. No wilderness is truly wild: every wilderness is affected by people, every wilderness affects people. Most wild areas have, through endless generations, had something to do with people. Much wilderness throughout the world has traditionally been everybody's, or nobody's. It was something to which no one, or everyone, had rights. To take a wilderness and to make it a reserve involves denying those rights, or the claiming of rights that had never previously existed. It involves changing, at a stroke, the history and tradition of centuries. This is not easily done.

Like all areas of wilderness, tiger country had always been a human resource. Tiger country was a place for hunting, gathering fuel, and often cattle grazing. Wilderness was essential to the life of many people. Different areas had different uses, and different emphases, but every wilderness has a human dimension. This is a rule that holds true all over the world: but it counts double and treble in ever more densely populated Asia. Inevitably, then, any attempts at imposing or denying rights over this land will disrupt lives and destroy communities.

India launched its own program for tiger conservation on April 1, 1973: Corbett National Park became the first Project Tiger reserve. Project Tiger was intended to be a dramatic, high-profile business. Dr Karan Singh, a son of the last Maharajah of Kashmir, was put in charge. It was an immensely complicated business. Forests and wildldife had always been the concern of state rather than central government. Singh and Sankhala pushed through legislation to make central government the partners of the individual states. This did not make state governments happy: it was estimated that the states, taken together, ceded control of an annual $14 million to central government.

Project Tiger was an immense business. Villages and entire communities were moved. Cattle were forbidden to roam the reserves. They were captured, impounded, and released only on payment of a fine. Grass burning, a traditional method of stimulating the growth of fresh grass for grazing domestic cattle, needed strict control. So did traditional activities like the gathering of firewood, the collection of grass for thatching, and the harvesting of wild honey.

The reserves also needed a buffer zone around them: a ring of good, if sub-optimal tiger habitat. This was particularly relevant for wandering male tigers, the nonbreeding population in waiting of potential territorial males. A managed reserve needs access for its many workers. Roads needed to be built, a time-consuming and expensive business, especially in remote areas. It was also essential to recruit, train, and deploy guards, to enforce the conditions of the reserves. Access was also important if tourism was to become a factor in Project Tiger. Tourism can be disruptive, but the industry has a peerless advantage of placing a clear dollar value on wildlife. This is true for both those at the top of the business food chain and for those nearer the bottom: tourism generates a good deal of local employment.

The sudden and dramatic steps to turn history on its head and to reverse the decline of the tiger made waves far beyond Asia. For a while it seemed that most of the world was carried away by enthusiasm. The thought of saving the tiger prompted a great rush of tiger-consciousness. In the West, money poured in to such organizations as the WWF. Private individuals did their bit; commercial concerns wanted to stand up and be counted - especially those that used a tiger as their symbol. Tiger skin became unacceptable to wear in civilized countries: there are reports of women booed in the streets for the wearing of tiger fur coats. Sophia Loren was asked hostile questions about her own tiger-skin coat: she replied that the seven tigers involved were already dead. Not everyone found this response as brilliant and as charming as she had hoped. In London a tiger coat was burnt in public. Even the armed forces of Britain got involved: the crew of HMS *Tiger* sent a donation to the fund. Military bands gave up the apron of real tiger skin that is traditionally worn by the bass drummer. These days, bass-drummers wear synthetic tiger-skin. Clothes made from artificial furs acquired both chic and street-cred. One by one, countries that had been consumers of tiger skins banned their import. In short, if good vibes had been tigers, then by the mid-1970s the world would have been overrun with stripy carnivores.

Good vibes led to good legislation.

Left:

AN ADULT MALE
TIGER STRIDES PAST
AT SUNSET IN
THE SECURITY OF
BANDHAVGARH
NATIONAL PARK,
INDIA.

Above:

THE IMPRESSIVE EFFORTS TO ESTABLISH TIGER RESERVES DID NOT AND COULD NOT AFFECT THE TRADE IN TIGERS' PARTS. HERE, TIGER BONES ARE SOLD OPENLY IN TAIWAN.

Another legislative triumph for conservation came with CITES, the Convention on Trade in Endangered Species of Fauna and Flora. This was an international agreement to refrain from trade in species that are, according to agreement between signing countries, in danger of extinction. Wildlife has always been a colossal item of trade: after all, there has always been plenty more where that came from. Looming extinction only affects trade by pushing the prices up, for the threat of extinction, as we have seen, makes the traded animal still more desirable. Wildife is the world's third largest illegal trade after drugs and arms; this does not take into account the huge volume of trade in wildlife that was, and still is, legal.

The initial agreement of CITES banned trade in tigers, alive, dead, or in bits. The signatories to CITES forbade, and in differing degrees enforced, the ban on trade in tigers and tigrine products. It began to become clear that the shock of the tiger's impending extinction had brought about a stunning and dramatic change in the world's thinking. The possibility of the extinction of the tiger woke the world up, not only to the tiger's own plight but, by implication, and because of the tiger's "sexiness", to the entire question of conservation. It seemed that the tiger was being saved: and that saving the tiger was helping to save everything else. Happy thought.

In India, nine tiger reserves were established, later rising to 21, and reports began to come in of booming tiger populations inside them. India basked in the pride of establishing a major and spectacularly succesful conservation project. In terms of international prestige, it seemed that a succesful national conservation policy was fast becoming second only to a national airline. Both showed the world that you were not a stagnant but a developing nation: a nation on the cutting edge of progress.

India remained the tiger's heartland and the centre of successful tiger conservation. Reports grew still better: some reserves stated that their tiger population had doubled. They explained this as a result of successful breeding, effective protection against poaching, and increasing numbers of prey animals. The success in India led to successes elsewhere. Malaysia, Thailand, and Indonesia wanted to create tiger reserves of their own. In 1980, China became a signatory to CITES. The government began to talk about conservation projects; three Chinese non-government organizations are members of the IUCN. It was further claimed that 150 Siberian tigers existed in China: a remarkable bonus. The Chinese said that there were relict populations of the Chinese tiger, and that these were now protected: there were also possibly tigers of the Indian and the Indochinese races. Reserves for tigers were now established in India, Bangladesh, Nepal, Bhutan, Malaysia, Thailand, Indonesia, the USSR, and China.

By 1979, ten years after the emergence of the killer-stat, a further census was completed. It gave a global figure of 6,400 for all races of tiger. The Indian tiger was now estimated at 3,300: over a thousand animals up on the killer-stat that had changed tigrine history. And that population, claimed reserve managers everywhere, was still growing. It was claimed without ambiguity that the tiger had been saved. It was a great landmark of conservation success. It all seemed too good to be true. And it was.

Right

EVEN AS THE WORLD
CELEBRATED THE
SUCCESS OF INDIA'S
PROJECT TIGER, A
SERIES OF NEW AND
DEADLY THREATS
BEGAN TO ASSAIL THE
WORLD'S TIGER
POPULATIONS.

WAR

on

TWO FRONTS

"You can say that there is now no danger of extinction of the tiger in India." So said B.R. Koppikar in 1980. He was then director of Project Tiger, the name chosen for India's massive tiger conservation master plan, which had been launched on Indira Gandhi's initiative in 1973. The conservation program that had been catapulted into such dynamic and flamboyant action by the then prime minister had grown and advanced. The advance had continued until India had established 21 Project Tiger reserves and invested $28 million in the project. It was an immense effort, one that put many wealthier countries to shame. And it was a great success.

India had unquestionably led the way. The tiger seemed to be the beneficiary of an unprecedented upsurge of international goodwill: goodwill from politicians, indeed people of all kinds. The world wanted the tiger to be saved: and it was saved. Now we could all relax and cheer.

But it was to become clear, as the 1980s gave way to the 1990s, that life was not so simple. Things had changed, but they were to change again. The tiger became caught in a pincer movement: a two-pronged attack that changed its global status once again.

For centuries it was a fact the tiger was a successful and populous animal. Almost too late, it was realized that the tiger was in truth on the edge of extinction. The great international effort cut in, and the tiger became a rescued animal: the animal that came back from the brink: a brilliant conservation success. But you cannot apply a hand-brake to history. In a matter of a few years it became clear that the tiger was in trouble once more: it was fighting a battle on two fronts and, once again, the tiger was staring extinction in the face. Once again humans must look at the tiger and come to terms with the overwhelming question of conservation: what sort of world do we wish to live in? What kind of world do we wish our grandchildren to live in?

The two-pronged assault on the tiger continues: both lines of attack are gathering pace and force. Neither is new, but their nature has changed. They are old enemies in different guises. The first is the old threat of ordinary, decent people trying to make a living: but the problems are worse, the threat more acute than before. In a continent of soaring population, life is more cramped than ever before and space is at an ever-higher premium. Any one who can find a solution, however short-term, to the problem of feeding family and children will inevitably take it. The second prong is the old enemy of direct persecution, but the reason for persecution has changed. Tigers are now killed not for the glee of the hunter, nor for political gain and agrarian reform, as was the case in the past. The new reason for killing tigers is rather more simple: money. People are willing to pay vast sums of money for bits of dead tiger. We will examine this phenomenon in a moment.

Deliberate persecution is one thing but, as we have already seen, the inadvertent pressures of an expanding human population cannot help but affect the tiger. Just about every wilderness area in the world is shrinking, nibbled away from the edges. Forests, rashly seen as renewable resources, are cut down for timber or cleared for agriculture, and are not, of course, renewed. The decline of moist Asian forests has been a helter-skelter business: from 1,291,000sq miles (3,345,000sq km) in 1980 to 1,110,000 sq miles (2,875,000sq km) in 1990, a loss of 18,000sq miles (47,000sq km) a year. This is not sustainable; and it is death to the tiger.

With forest destruction comes fragmentation. Increasingly, tiger populations are confined to small islands of wilderness in a rising sea of humanity.

Left:

FORESTRY IS SUPPOSED
TO BE A "RENEWABLE
RESOURCE" BUT
THE PACE OF
DESTRUCTION HAS
OUTSTRIPPED THAT OF
REGENERATION BY A
DISTANCE. MUCH OF
ASIAN FORESTRY IS
WHOLESALE HABITAT
DESTRUCTION.

These islands themselves are being eroded by surging tides of people, their crops, their cattle and goats. In India, the reserves of Corbett and Rajaji, once linked, are virtually separated. The same is true of Kanha and Bandhavgarh, though here the break could be repaired. Other reserves have been cut off from the forests they once abutted.

It is worth looking a little more closely at Project Tiger. India's great conservation project has been seen in turn as one of the great conservation success stories of our time, a template for all future projects; then subsequently as one of the great conservation disasters. Neither is

quite fair. Without the great international impact made by Project Tiger, it is possible that the tiger would now be extinct. If the mistakes made by the project seem obvious in hindsight, they are mistakes from which all conservation bodies have learnt.

The Project Tiger reserves were established by creating tigers-only areas, not an easy matter in a densely populated country. The solution was draconian: a large number of the people who lived in the newly designated reserve areas were moved out. Entire villages were relocated by the decree of central government: about 100,000 people in all were shunted along. It was, in its way, a spectacular logistical achievment, one performed under a whole-hearted commitment to conservation. Its guiding philosophy was the thought that you can't make an omelette without breaking eggs. It must be said that the task of relocating people is performed in much more spectacular numbers for major "development" and industrial projects. In all such forced relocations, the evicted people themselves could be forgiven if they believed that the government had adopted the plenty-more-where-that-came-from philosophy, in relation to poor farmers and their families. If the tigers' displaced neighbours felt no animosity to the tigers themselves, they certainly felt that something less than loving cooperation was due towards governments, civil servants and conservationists. They were moved on because of the tiger, but they were given no stake, financial or emotional, in the tiger's future. They were moved on with promises of improved health care, new wells and so on: when these failed to materialize, the string of broken promises was added to the trauma of eviction. It was not the best way of making friends for tigers.

The initial notion of Project Tiger was magnificent. The method of implementing it was less so. This was the case not only in the heartless "tigers first" method of establishing the reserves, but also in a widening gap between ambition and performance. This is a constant bane of conservation: the difference between theory and practise. Making a fine public show of saving the tiger is one thing: but the detailed nitty-gritty of the business, delegated through layer upon layer of subordinates, and performed in what are necessarily remote and difficult places, may well not live up to the high ideals and brave talk of the founders.

It is in some ways unfair to single out Project Tiger for criticism. Project Tiger made a braver step than any other conservation initiative to safeguard the tiger's future. Project Tiger was the biggest, most courageous, and unquestionably the most effective attempt the world has ever seen to safeguard the future of the tiger. Other nations that took less ambitious, less optimistic steps have not made such noticeable errors. They avoided errors by the simple method of not trying half as hard to save the tigers in the first place.

But in its failure to bring local people onto the side of conservation, Project Tiger suffered. When it came down to the details of administration, desire in New Delhi did not lead inexorably to performance in the jungle. Park boundaries are vague, and their status in law has never been made perfectly clear. The Forest Department is actually felling timber in a number of reserves; a bus service crosses another reserve; quarrying takes place inside the boundaries of a third. In many ways, Project Tiger is in a confused and muddled situation.

And since the tumultuous launching of Project Tiger, it has slipped as a priority. Rajiv Gandhi maintained Project Tiger as a priority when he took over as Prime Minister after the assassination of his mother. Subsequent governments have

AS HUMAN POPULA-
TIONS INCREASE AND
SPREAD, THEY INVADE
AREAS TIGERS ONCE
HAD TO THEMSELVES,
WITH INEVITABLE
TENSIONS BETWEEN
BOTH POPULATIONS.
HERE A TIGER FEASTS
ON DOMESTIC CATTLE.

not kept up this momentum, and have always lacked the Gandhis' personal involvement. The post of field director of a Project Tiger reserve is not everybody's dream of a plum job. For the purely ambitious, it is something of a backward promotion. One reserve had seven directors in six years. There are, it must be said, many impressive and dedicated people remaining in conservation in India. But they have lost the sympathy of central government. Such men are no longer valued as they should be: they have lost the support and patronage of the Prime Minister's office.

Government decisions, and the assessment of the performance of government employees, are matters that are carried out in offices, not jungles. Top people in government and civil service do not creep about the forest counting tigers. They just need the figures on their desks. But as we know, the problems of tiger census are immense: it is virtually impossible to produce truly accurate figures for tiger populations. How many field directors even tried? In New Delhi, they wanted good news: they got it by the barrowload.

No one wanted to be the bearer of a bad tidings. Project Tiger continued in its gloriously bullish way, but increasingly in the face of the facts. From 1990, in Ranthambhore, tigers well known to park staff were no longer sighted. It was speculated that this was merely a change in behavior: tourist pressure had made the tigers more elusive. But in the reserve itself, there was still concern. A tiger census was completed in 1992. It came up with a population of 15, perhaps 20 tigers; compare this with 44 in 1989. The state government of Rajasthan pooh-poohed this census, and abused the people who performed it. Central government played down any suggestion that tigers were being poached.

In November 1992 the Cat Specialist Group of the IUCN met in Delhi to discuss tiger populations. There was no longer any ducking the matter: we were back in the familiar scenario of crisis. The Indian government took this fact on board at an international forum on the tiger in 1993. The Indian Minister for environment and forests, Kamal Nath, proposed that a Global Tiger Forum should be established. This met for the first time in March 1994, with representatives of 11 of the 14 range states of the tiger.

It is now conjectured that many field directors deliberately bumped up their tiger figures in an understandable desire to keep central government, and Mrs Gandhi, happy. High figures showed that the field director was doing a good job: back in New Delhi, they showed that everybody in New Delhi was doing a good job too. Everyone was happy. Project Tiger marched into the 1980s in a mood of euphoria, not to say self-congratulation. Any one who criticized the project was singing a song no one wanted to hear. It was in this fashion that complacency became the enemy within.

But the greatest of the disasters to affect Project Tiger was not the fault of the project at all. It was the fact that over 20 years the Indian population rose by 50 per cent. People pressure means agricultural pressure, with increases in grazing and fuel gathering. The forests were and are being destroyed by the people who live around them. In fact, they are being destroyed by the people who love and cherish them most. There are further problems, and still greater ones, with the peripheral areas, the buffer zones that surround the reserves. Fuelwood and timber is demanded by more and more people, further and further from the forests. Thus fuel, once gathered for subsistence, has become a business commodity. Reserve managers say that it is quite impossible for local people to find firewood anywhere other than on protected sites: naturally, they go onto protected sites. Children, not

tigers, are their priority.

There are several morals to be drawn from Project Tiger. The first is that in no project, let alone a conservation project, is it enough simply to make a good start. A second moral is that any conservation effort that operates counter to the will of local people is doomed. This is a lesson that has been taken on board in conservation projects across the world. More and more wildlife projects are now community-orientated. To take one random example, a conservation project in a small tract of unique forest in Africa incorporated, as part of its conservation work, a close and intense relationship with the local community as a first priority. This even included the building of a

Left:

GOOD HEALTH AND LONG LIFE, THOUGH NOT TO TIGERS: A SELECTION OF CHINESE TIGER-BASED MEDICINES AND ELIXIRS.

football pitch and the establishment of a local football team. When the Clarke's Weavers - they are named after a species of bird that is found only in that tract of forest, and they play in a strip that mimics its black and yellow plumage - go into action, they are fighting a blow for conservation. This project, and many like it, has learnt hugely from the mistakes of Project Tiger.

Conservation may start as a form of idealism, but practical conservation is a matter of very hard labor and intense involvement in politics. Political problems flock around the tiger like carrion birds around a tiger kill. In India the infiltration of tiger reserves by guerrilla groups has meant the surrender of control over those areas. After all, wildernesses have been traditional havens for outlaws ever since there were laws to flee from. Robin Hood and Sikh extremists both took traditional routes to avoid the forces of authority. It is reckoned that seven, perhaps eight tiger reserves are affected by guerrillas. These groups have taken advantage of poor administration and negligible enforcement of the law, and have succeeded in making both these things utterly impossible in their chosen areas. A logging mafia is involved with one park; in another, 12 forest guards were killed and the field director now needs a police escort to get into his own area. In four more reserves the Naxalites, a Maoist group, have used local resentment at the high-handed approach of Project Tiger as a means of attracting support.

Again, we must be wary of singling

Left:

POPULATION PRES-
SURES: DECLINING
GOVERNMENT
AUTHORITY IN NEPAL
HAS PERMITTED PEO-
PLE TO EXPLOIT AREAS
THAT HAD PREVIOUSLY
BEEN SAFEGUARDED
FOR TIGERS.

Right:

THE ULTIMATE
APHRODISIAC: A TIGER
PENIS ON SALE IN
HARBIN, CHINA.

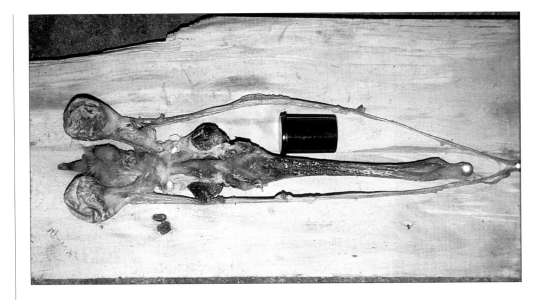

India out. Similar problems affect wilderness areas the world over. In India, the world's most populous democracy, such matters are a matter of public concern and public debate. Here all disasters are in the public domain.

In Nepal, a change of government in 1991 has led to a decline in the authority of army and police, and therefore there is greater opportunity for local people to exploit the protected areas for firewood, and for the poaching of rhinoceros and tiger. Central authority in IndoCchina, following decades of war, has left wilderness areas without effective protection. In China, a weakening of authority in the south has encouraged freelance, as opposed to government-backed tiger killers, and they are killing tigers for profit. The Chinese government says that it has executed seven people in five years for "crimes against tigers."

Perhaps the biggest political problem facing the tiger has been the breakup of the Soviet Union. These days, the plight of the Siberian tiger is at the top of few people's lists of priorities although many conservationists are swinging against the tide manfully. And that means that for a long period there will be little or nothing to stop poachers poaching. More recently, international funds and assistance has been introduced to the far east of the former Soviet Union; but the situation, though improved, is still chaotic.

But at least half of the tiger's political problems can be simplified dramatically. We have seen that the tiger is under a two-pronged attack: by the inadvertent assault of an expanding human population, and by direct persecution. Until the beginning of the 1970s direct persecution was largely a matter of hunting, or, in the case of the Caspian and the Chinese tigers, a government-inspired program to eradicate a "pest". But direct persecution has been stepped up in recent years, because there has been an unprecedented demand for dead tigers as a commercial product.

The inequality of wealth is an ineluctable fact of global politics. The rich - people, families, nations, hemispheres - can have anything they like from the poor. All they need offer in return is money, and for the rich, there is plenty more where that came from. Most tigers live in poor countries; in richer countries, a lot of people want dead tigers. Inevitably, then, tigers are killed and sold to the rich, while a series of middlemen take their cut.

What does the world want with dead tigers? As we have seen, the tiger has a powerful hold on the culture and the imagination and on the hearts and minds of the world, in the West as in the East. This has inspired the great conservation efforts: it has also led to great destruction of tigers. In the Arab countries there are people willing to pay serious money for tiger skins. Where wealth equals virility, so the tiger becomes a symbol of virility, and by this cockeyed process of reasoning the possession of a tiger skin becomes a status symbol of rare potency. Looming extinction only makes a tiger-skin more desirable, and confers more status and by implication, more potency than ever before.

But the trade in skins is for the dealers only a tasty bonus. The real boom has come in the unprecedented demand for tiger products. Bits of dead tiger are used in traditional Chinese medicines. The philosophy here is ancient, but the size of the demand for tigers relatively new. The consumption of tiger bones is said to be a cure for rheumatism, and it is supposed to be an aid to a longer life. Tiger-bone wine is valued as something close to an elixir of life. Tiger whiskers are thought to contain potent poisons, or alternatively to confer great strength. Pills made from tiger's eyes allegedly prevent convulsions. And best of all, you cannot beat a nice bowl of tiger's penis soup if you wish to bolster a flagging libido. It is said that affluent Chinese will happily pay $320 for this delicacy.

There is money, then, in bits of dead tiger: very serious money. And despite the laws and treaties that ban trade in tigers, a largely illegal industry has sprung from this demand. A tiger skin can fetch up to $15,000, but this aspect of the trade is not without risks: a tiger's skin is, after

Below:

A WINDOW DISPLAY TO ATTRACT THE PUNTERS: A TIGER'S SKULL ADVERTIZES A SHOP SELLING TIGER-BASED MEDICINES IN TAIWAN.

Opposite:

HUNTING IN SIBERIA
CONTINUES EVEN
THOUGH THE TIGER IS
AN INTERNATIONALLY
PROTECTED SPECIES.
SMALL GROUPS OF
TRACKERS WHO
CATCH YOUNG TIGERS
WITH THEIR BARE
HANDS STILL EXIST.
AFTER THE TIGER HAS
BEEN SURROUNDED BY
BARKING DOGS, THE
HUNTERS PIN DOWN
THE ANIMAL WITH
THEIR FORKLIKE
STICKS. THE TIGER IS
THEN BUNDLED UP
QUICKLY, AS THE
HUNTERS
FEAR THE RETURN OF
THE YOUNG TIGER'S
MOTHER.

all, somewhat recognizable. Tiger-bones and other tiger parts can easily be passed off as something else.

The taste for tiger products lies deep in Chinese mythology and culture. The Chinese government's determination to eradicate the Chinese tiger in the 1960s created a glut of dead tigers, and therefore an extraordinary opportunity to create, sell and experiment with tiger products. By the middle of the 1980s the stockpile of tiger bones was dwindling, but the demand for tiger products stayed the same. And with the increasing rarity and expense of these products, the demand soared.

In China, Taiwan, Hong Kong, and Korea, wealthy and powerful people wanted tigers. They wanted to live longer, to increase their sexual power: in short, to live forever and to copulate eternally. They held the belief, which no amount of scientific proof to the contrary could shake, that the tiger would help them achieve this glorious dream. It was tough on the tiger, of course, but for a matter as important as this, it was clear that something had to give.

Thus, as air rushes in to fill a vacuum, poachers rushed in to meet the soaring demand for tiger products. Where there is big money for illegal demands, undercover organizations spring up. The organization TRAFFIC, was established to monitor the world's trade in wildlife on behalf of the Worldwide Fund for Nature. The Organization set up undercover operations, and revealed a large poaching trade in Delhi. In a single raid police in

New Delihi found 850lb (385kg) of tiger bones, reckoned to be what was left of 42 tigers. But any judicial system in the world is amenable to the manipulation of the rich and powerful, and India is no exception to that rule. Quick and successful prosecutions of people involved in the tiger trade have not materialized.

There are estimates that in India alone, 500 tigers have been poached between 1991 and 1994; some put this as high as 1,000. When you consider that estimates, in fact estimates widely considered to have been inflated, placed the Indian tiger population at around 3,000, the extent of the problem becomes clear.

Once again India is at the center of attention. Not only is India considered the tiger nation but, as said before, its problems are inevitably, democratically, in the public domain. In Siberia the situation is still worse. The Siberian tiger's heartland, an area known as the taiga, was formerly under the tight control of the Soviet state. Now, with the breakup of the Soviet Union, control has gone. It is said that the poacher now controls the taiga. It is reckoned that if this situation remains unchanged, the Siberian tiger will cease to have a viable breeding population by 1997. After that, it can only be a long, slow wind-down to extinction.

It cannot be denied that these problems seem unstoppable. The problems of direct persecution can be attacked from two ends. From one end it seems that neither direct protection of the tigers, nor any attempt at controlling the poachers, has done much good. Clearly,

the tiger needs something close to a revolution in anti-poaching enforcement. The second line of approach is to control the end users. It is not a simple matter. To do so would be to require the Koreans and the Chinese to turn their backs on several millennia of culture and tradition. If the apple was an endangered fruit, would Americans give in to a world demand that they refrain from eating apple pie? Or would they offer huge sums in dollars for smuggled apples from the last orchards of the third world? Would the British government cave into a global demand and prevent its citizens from consuming fish and chips? (For that matter, there is a global crisis over fisheries.) It is clear then, that in this matter of the tiger, we are faced with a thumping great cultural collision. All these tiger-consuming countries have signed agreements on conservation and the wildlife trade: their efforts to enforce them have been notable for remorseless efficiency.

South Korea openly and legally traded in tiger parts until July 1993. In the final year the volume of trade rose sharply: a move naturally interpreted as the stockpiling of tiger products in anticipation of

Right:

THE TIGER TRADE IN FULL SWING: A TIGER IS SKINNED BEFORE GOING TO AUCTION IN TAIWAN, TO THE DELIGHT OF THE TRADERS.

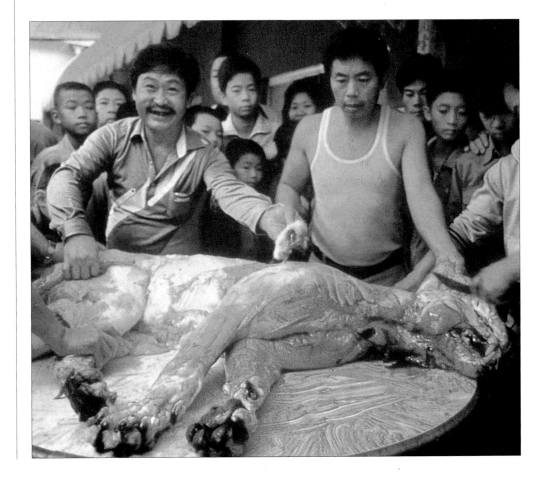

a ban. In 1993 South Korea became a signatory to CITES, the Convention on Trade in Endangered Species. But it has not prevented the sale of tiger products within its borders. However, the sale of tiger bones in South Korea will be banned in November 1994 and derivatives, including drugs from March 1995. Although this is certainly a great leap forward, the nationwide will to enforce the ban is a different matter.

Taiwan has had legal measures to prohibit the sale of tiger products for 15 years. But there is, to put it mildly, a lack of political will to enforce this. The London-based Environmental Investigation Agency (EPA) has produced evidence to show that the sale of tiger products has continued openly. In response to the fuss the organization managed to kick up, tiger products were taken off the shelves of traditional Taiwanese pharmacies. But inevitably, subsequent investigations showed that the sale continues: the only change is a minimal discretion over the sale. Since April 1994, and the US Government enforced sanctions upon Taiwan; the Taiwanese government has cracked down on the sale of tiger bones.

There are further worries about this situation: worries that go beyond tigers. It is possible that, once the demand for tiger parts has driven the tiger into extinction, the focus of attention for the consumers of these elixirs of life will shift to the other big cats of the world. Already snow leopards, whose stronghold is Tibet, have become part of the bone trade. Leopard and golden cat bones have also been used as substitutes for tiger bones in Chinese medicine. All species of big cat have a potential part to play in this search for long life and lots of sex. It is likely that demand could shift from tigers, once they are extinct, to lion and leopard. The craze for the consumption of animal parts has already brought all five of the world's species of rhinoceros to the brink of extinction. As we have seen, the tiger is now fast approaching the same state. The endless, fruitless quest for eternal youth could wipe out species as yet unthreatened.

The situation, then, is grim. There is no getting away from that. However, it is also true that the ultimate conservation crime is despair. That helps neither man nor tiger. It is time now to move on and look at hope.

Right

CONSERVATIONISTS
SAY TIGERS MUST BE
SAVED. THIS PICTURE
OF RANTHAMBHORE
TIGERS DOES A GOOD
JOB OF EXPLAINING
WHY.

TWENTY-FIRST
CENTURY
TIGER

THE TIGER CAN BE SAVED. THIS IS EMPHATICALLY NOT CUSTER'S LAST STAND, WHERE DEFEAT IS INEVITABLE AND THE ONLY OPTION REMAINING IS TO GO DOWN BRAVELY. THE SAVING OF THE TIGER IS NOT A PIOUS HOPE, IT IS STILL A REAL POSSIBILITY. JUST ABOUT. FOR IT WILL BE AN APPALLINGLY DIFFICULT BUSINESS. WE ARE LOSING TIGERS AT THE RATE OF TWO A DAY. THAT FIGURE IS STARTLING; BUT IT OWES SOMETHING TO GUESSWORK. OTHERS SUGGEST FIGURES BETWEEN ONE AND FIVE A DAY. WHATEVER THE EXACT FIGURE, IT IS FAR, FAR TOO MANY. BUT SAVING THE TIGER IS POSSIBLE: CONSERVATION IS NOT SPITTING INTO THE WIND, IT IS MERELY TAKING ON AN EXTREMELY DIFFICULT TASK IN THE FACE OF CONSIDERABLE ODDS. IT CAN BE DONE.

Conservation must fight a war on many fronts, in the knowledge that victory in many areas and many aspects of life will be close to impossible. But all the battles will contribute to the main struggle, and a number of victories may possibly be achieved.

The problem of tiger consumption has propelled the tiger into crisis, and the task of quelling the demand of the tiger-consuming nations looks impossible. Certainly, the threat of trade sanctions, the attempt to put more teeth into the CITES agreement and the work of investigation agencies are required to marginalize the trade as far as possible. The problem is not in CITES itself, but in the enforcement it demands. In many of the tiger's range countries there is no legal or administrative structure for its enforcement. Education and an attempt to summon up the political will in the consumer countries are relevant and important matters. Perhaps the crucial issue is that of political will.

But all this won't actually stop the trade. It can only drive it deeper underground. As long as there are people in China, Taiwan, Hong Kong and Korea who believe that from bits of dead tiger an elixir of life can be created, that threat will remain, pushing tigers towards extinction. Measures to control this will apply the brake; they will slow down, but cannot actually halt the juggernaut of destruction.

Political will remains a major problem in the consumer states, and also in the states where tigers still actually live. The 1994 meeting of the Global Tiger Forum was represented by virtually all the countries in the tiger's

Right:

TIGER AUCTION IN TAIWAN: AN UNMITIGATED HORROR SHOW. REGULAR SCENES IN THE 1980s, AUCTIONS ARE NOW ILLEGAL. ALTHOUGH THIS IS A STEP IN THE RIGHT DIRECTION, THIS LEGISLATION HAS FORCED SUCH AUCTIONS UNDERGROUND.

range, and they all agreed to make all kinds of strong commitments to the drawing up of a national strategy for tiger conservation, each one complete with targets and costs. Pious lip service will not save tigers, nor is it supposed to do. The right things were said, but what will actually happen? Again, it depends on political will. How many countries believe that merely saying the right things is enough? How many see talk-shops as a way of shutting up the critics? And how many will initiate or escalate pro-tiger action?

The fact is that the trend of habitat loss, through deliberate tree-felling programs and the inadvertent but inevitable advance of local populations, will continue in virtually all the range states of the tiger. Rather than move depressingly from one country's problems and inaction to the next, let us turn to the places where the tiger's long-term future looks most promising.

Myanmar is one. There is still plenty of good habitat. But also the poaching of tigers continues, with a trade route into Thailand. The military government is an equivocal ally. To speak purely in terms of tiger conservation, such a government can impose draconian measures, and even enforce them in the areas of the country over which it has full control. There is a largely uncontrolled border with China, however, where illicit wildlife trade has long been a fact of life. The long-term stability of a military government is a more uncertain matter; should it fall, resentment at its decrees is inevitable. Nor has the country demonstrated much political will for conservation. Myanmar has a hint of possibilities, but little more than that.

Siberia has attracted a great deal of gloom-and-doom mongering about the tiger. Certainly, it is a fact that with the collapse of the Soviet Union, authority has gone from the tiger habitat, and poaching is rife. But the point is that in trying to combat poaching in Siberia (and in much of Asia), you are not fighting on a broad front. You are fighting on an extremely narrow front, against an enemy who is pretty clearly defined. The problem is not that half the population of Siberia is shooting and selling tigers. Poaching is in the hands of a small number of Russian gangs. The dynamics of poaching are such that investigation can expose the people behind it. Enforcement could, almost at a stroke, dramatically reduce poaching. This is not happening at the moment, and tiger numbers are being reduced very quickly indeed. There are further problems: humans are killing wild pigs for food, depriving tigers of a vital prey. There is also a new problem of habitat destruction: logging concessions have been granted to corporations from United States and South Korea.

But the Siberian tiger can be saved: it is an achievable goal. The pressure of human population on tiger habitat in Siberia is very slight. That is something that makes Siberia, in all the tiger's range, more or less unique. The wilderness awaits the possibility of a tigrine resurgence in Siberia.

There are two types of human population that are capable of living in harmony with tigers. The first population is simply a very low one; the Siberian option. The second is a population that is deeply committed to the saving of the tiger. That is the Indian option. India has an ever-expanding population, but in that extraordinary country there is, despite the pressure of people, a deep commitment to nature, to animals, to life in every aspect it appears on earth. This is, perhaps, an aspect of the Hindu religion: the least people-centered major religion on earth.

Poaching is a problem in India as it is in Siberia, but again, it is a a battle on a narrow front. And it is not a local business: the local communities get nothing from tiger poachers. Tiger poachers are rich outsiders, city slickers, and they come to plunder an area and go. Poachers, and most particularly the successful middlemen, are therefore deeply resented by local people: outsiders and foreigners robbing them of their tigers. There is a story of a poacher arriving in a Mercedes, buying a goat from local people as a bait, and then setting off to bag his tiger and reap his profit. The villagers set the car on fire and arrested the poacher. True, the poacher paid the usual bribe and got away; but the incident, and many others like it, shows profound opposition to the poachers. This is not merely resentment at the crooked and successful: it is also a strong groundswell of feeling for tigers.

With tigers, every hint of optimisim must be tempered with caution. The clandestine trade in India continues to run smoothly, with the poisoning of tiger kills, trapping and shooting. Arrested poachers and dealers tend to get off with a small fine.

"India is full of a latent desire to protect tigers," said Robin Pellew, director of the British arm of the WWF. "Many people there have a strong desire to see the tiger and the forest survive: they actively want to play the guardian role. It is something that is very, very deeply felt. It is a spiritual matter. The Hindu religion is a very strong force for conservation. That is an advantage that the tiger has only in India. With it comes a commitment to and an understanding of the forest and the tiger. The country also has two-thirds of the world's tigers. These things are what make India the best long-term bet for the future of the tiger."

This is a matter as fragile as it is splendid, and it is something no one dares to take for granted. Optimism on this score has to be treated with circumspection. For a start, some of the communities that might have delighted in a "guardian" role were treated roughly in the early days of Project Tiger: kicked out of their ancestral villages so that tiger reserves could be created. Rather more importantly, with the current unending and tumultuous economic growth across the developing world, many young Indians look to a romantic dream of the future and of American-style commerce, rather than to their roots and their parents' values. It is not just tigers and the forests that are passing through a period of crisis and change.

Hindu goodwill does not have to stand alone as the last safeguard of the

Left:

AS HANDSOME AND AS
WELL-ARMED AS EVER:
BUT THE TIGER'S
TRADITIONAL
WEAPONS COUNT FOR
NOTHING AS THE
BATTLE AGAINST
EXTINCTION
CONTINUES.

Right:

IN BENARES, ONE OF
THE GREAT SPIRITUAL
CENTERS OF INDIA, A
TIGER DOMINATES THE
URBAN SKYLINE. THE
INDIAN SPIRITUAL
AFFINITY WITH THE
TIGER IS A CLEAR RAY
OF HOPE IN A MURKY
DISTURBED WORLD.

Right:

IN BENARES, ONE OF
THE GREAT SPIRITUAL
CENTERS OF INDIA, A
TIGER DOMINATES THE
URBAN SKYLINE. THE
INDIAN SPIRITUAL
AFFINITY WITH THE
TIGER IS A CLEAR RAY
OF HOPE IN A MURKY
DISTURBED WORLD.

tiger. For a start, in addition to this spiritual and ancestral goodwill to all tigers, there is the phenomenon of what is termed "ecodevelopment." This is essentially a strategy of conservation that places people first on the agenda. A classic example goes like this.

The local population has always relied on the forest for feeding their cattle and as a source of fuel. But the forest is disappearing under the ever greater pressures of an increasing human population: neither the forest, not the people's way of life, is sustainable. Cattle with a higher yield of milk are introduced. Land is managed to grow dry season fodder for them: thus there is no need to cut browse from the forest. This fodder is fed to the cattle in stalls. The cattle dung in the same place, and their droppings can be gathered easily. From dung comes biogas, which provides fuel for cooking. Thus people do not need to go to the forest to cut fuel; both forest and community can survive.

There are projects like this all over the world. India is crammed with self-help projects: health and education are primary goals, but conservation is seen increasingly as a matter that is not only important, but very much a local concern. The notion of the sustainable forest is returning to the realms of the possible.

"The tiger must be seen as a global symbol of biodiversity," said Valmik Thapar, the Indian tiger expert. "We need to harness the international will to save the tiger: we want to see a global commitment to the tiger's future. Also, we need the belief and the commitment of the range states of the tiger, the support of the local communities. We need politicians to understand that political rhetoric will not save the tiger. Resources, commitment, political will. If we cannot save the tiger, we can save nothing.

"We have looked at some of the many contradictions that swarm around tigers: the ferocious beast and the peaceful avoider of conflict; the loner and the lover of family life; the beast that people worshipped and the beast that people have persecuted without mercy; the lord of the jungle and the outcast whose jungle is being destroyed; an animal greatly feared yet an animal still more greatly loved. We are left with the final contradiction of conservation: that essential dualism of lofty, even spiritual idealism, and the sordid nitty-gritty of practical politics. Tigers still dwell in the realm of the possible. It is possible that the combination of idealism and hard politicking, at local and international level, can keep alive that strange, contradictory relationship between people and tigers. We need to keep the tiger alive. It is something we owe. We owe it to the tigers themselves: we owe it to life: we owe it to ourselves; we owe it to our grandchildren."

The tiger's future does not entirely depend on governments and organizations: these must be seen as conduits, albeit clogged, leaking and otherwise unreliable, of the people's will. The fate of the tiger lies in the hands of people: in the hands of millions and millions of individuals. Those of the tiger's range states in which tigers still have a great part to play; those who live close to the tigers have the greatest part to play of all. Those of us who live in developed countries, where the mistakes of previous generations have done much to destroy the wildlife and in particular, the great big enthralling animals, have a part to play as well in the galvanizing of global will to save the tiger. Such will is best expressed by involvement with conservation organizations, expressing the will for the tiger's survival by donating a little money, perhaps even a little time. It is a way of standing up to be counted: to cast a vote in favor of tigers, in favor of conservation, in favor of life.

The survival of the tiger has become a question about the human spirit. The tiger, once dependent merely on jungles and and prey animals, now finds that its entire future depends on human nature. There is as much contradiction here as there is in any tiger. The tiger stands on the cusp of extinction, yet the tiger can be saved.

BIBLIOGRAPHY

Jet Bakels, "The Tiger by the Tail: On tigers, ancestors and nature spirits in Kerinci," *Tiger Beat*, Minnesota Zoo, July 1993.

William Blake, *The Songs of Experience* and *The Marriage of Heaven and Hell*, ed. J. Bronowski, Penguin, 1958.

Paul Colinvaux, *Why Big Fierce Animals Are Rare*, George Allen and Unwin, 1980.

J.C. Cooper, *Symbolic and Mythological Animals*, Aquarian Press, 1992.
— (ed.), *Brewer's Myth and Legend*, Cassell, 1992.

Charles Darwin, *Of the Origin of Species by Means of Natural Selection...*, John Murray, 1859 (many reprints).

Richard Dawkins, *The Selfish Gene*, Oxford University Press, new edn 1989.
— *The Blind Watchmaker*, Longman, 1989.

J.G. Frazer, *The Golden Bough: A Study in Magic and Religion*, Macmillan, 1890-1915, rev. edn 1922.

Stephen Jay Gould, *Ever Since Darwin*, Burnett, 1978.
— *The Panda's Thumb*, W.W. Norton, 1980.
— *The Flamingo's Smile*, W.W. Norton, 1985.
— *Time's Arrow, Time's Cycle*, Harvard University Press, 1987.

— *An Urchin in the Storm*, W.W. Norton, 1987.
— *Wonderful Life,* Hutchinson Radius, 1989.
— *Bully for Brontosaurus*, Hutchinson Radius, 1991.
— *Eight Little Piggies*, W.W. Norton, 1993.

Robert Graves, *The White Goddess: A historical grammar of poetic myth*, Faber, 1961.

Donald R. Griffin, *Animal Thinking*, Harvard University Press, 1984.

Peter Jackson, *The Status of the Tiger in 1993*, report to Cat Specialist Group of International Union for Conservation of Nature and Natural Resources, 1993.
— Article in *BBC Wildlife* magazine, November 1989.
— *Endangered Species: Tigers*, Apple Press, 1990.

K. Ullas Karanth, "Analysis of Predator-Prey Balance in Bandipur Tiger Reserve with reference to census reports," *Journal of Bombay Natural History Society*, April 1988.

Francis X. King, *The Encyclopaedia of Mind, Magic and Mysteries*, Dorling Kindersley, 1991.

Rudyard Kipling, *The Jungle Book*, Macmillan, 1894.
—, *The Second Jungle Book*, Macmillan, 1895.

Eugene Linden, article in *Time* magazine, March 28, 1994.

Charles McDougal, *The Face of the Tiger*, Rivington, 1977.

Donald A. Mackenzie, *Indian Myth and Legend*, Gresham, 1913.

Jeffrey A. McNeely and Paul Spencer Wachtel, *Soul of the Tiger: Searching for Nature's Answers in Southeast Asia*, Oxford University Press, 1991, originally published as *Soul of the Tiger: Searching for Nature's Answers in Exotic Southeast Asia*, Doubleday, New York, 1988.

Aubrey Manning, *An Introduction to Animal Behaviour*, Edward Arnold, 1979.

Mary Midgeley, *Animals and Why They Matter*, University of Georgia Press, 1983.

Stephen Mills, articles in *BBC Wildlife* magazine January 1994 and November 1992.

A.A. Milne, *The House at Pooh Corner*, Methuen and Co., 1928.

Guy Mountford, *Saving the Tiger*, Michael Joseph, 1981.

Wendy Doniger O'Flaherty, *Sexual Metaphors and Animal Symbols in Hindu Mythology*, University of Chicago Press 1980.
— *The Origins of Evil in Hindu Mythology*, University of California Press, 1976.

Alexander Pope, *Poetical Works*, Oxford University Press, 1966.

T I G E R !

J.R. Porter and W.M.S. Russell, *Animals in Folklore*, D.S. Brewer, 1978.

Harriet Ritvo, *The Animal Estate*, Penguin, 1987.

John Seidensticker and Charles Macdougal, "Tiger Predatory Behaviour and Conservation," article in *Symposium of the Zoological Society of London*, 1993.

Kailash Sankhala, *Tiger! The Story of the Indian Tiger*, Collins, 1978.

George B. Schaller, *The Serengeti Lion*, University of Chicago Press, 1972.

Peter Singer, *In Defence of Animals*, Basil Blackwell, 1985.
— *Animal Liberation*, New York Review of Books, 2nd edn, 1990.

Arjan Singh, *Tiger! Tiger!*, Jonathan Cape, 1984.

Madeline K. Sprind, *Animal Allegories in T'ang China*, American Oriental Society, 1993.

Fiona and Mel Sunquist, *Tiger Moon*, University of Chicago Press, 1988.

Valmik Thapar, *Tigers: The Secret Life*, Elm Tree Books, 1989.

Geoffrey C. Ward, *Tiger Wallahs: Encounters with the men who tried to save the greatest of the great cats*, HarperCollins, 1993.

TIGER PROJECTS

The world's leading conservation organizations.

World Wide Fund for Nature (WWF) UK
Panda House
Weyside Park
Godalming
Surrey GU7 1XR
United Kingdom

World Wide Fund for Nature (WWF) Germany
Hedderichstr. 10
PO Box 701127
6000
Frankfurt a/M 70
Germany

World Wide Fund for Nature (WWF) USA
1250 24th Street NW
Washington DC
20037-1175
USA

TRAFFIC India
Ashok Kumar (Director)
172-B Lodi Estate
New Delhi 110003
India

Global Tiger Patrol
PO Box 100
Corsham
Hants
PO6 4TU
United Kingdom

The Tiger Trust
Chevington
Bury St Edmonds
Suffolk IP29 5RG
United Kingdom

The twice yearly publication *Cat News* is available for Swiss Francs 45 per year from:

Peter Jackson
Chairman
IUCN Cat Specialist Group
1172 Bougy
Switzerland

Please make payments to the Cat Specialist Group

INDEX

PICTURE ACKNOWLEDGEMENTS

Ancient Art and Architecture Collection 72-73, 80; © Keith Bernstein/Frank Spooner Pictures 93, 96-97, 103, 140-141; Jeremy Bradshaw 7; © The British Museum, London 87, 88, 89; Alain Compost/Bruce Coleman Ltd 71, 108; Eric Crichton/Bruce Coleman Ltd 92; Gerald Cubitt/Bruce Coleman Ltd 28, 121, 122; M. Day/The Tiger Trust Picture Library 20, 27, 29, 65, 66, 69, 130, 142, 143; M. & S. Day/The Tiger Trust Picture Library 107; S. Day/The Tiger Trust Picture Library 119, 135, 139; Sue Earle/Planet Earth Pictures 12, 42, 43, 44; Mary Evans Picture Library 78, 79, 81, 82, 86, 90, 91, 94, 98, 100; P.J.

Griffiths/Magnum 111; Daniel Heuclin/NHPA 39; Hulton Deutsch Collection Ltd 99, 118; Images of India 79; Peter F.R. Jackson/Bruce Coleman Ltd 15, 68; E.A. Kuttapan 31, 38, 45, 51, 52, 54, 59, 70, 116-117, 123, 125, 126, 132-133, 137, 153; Gerard Lacz/NHPA 40, 41; Ken Lucas/Planet Earth Pictures 63; Peter Marlow/Magnum 109; Fred Mayer/Magnum 145; Natural History Museum, London 62; Raghu Rai/Magnum 64, 75, 76, 101, 154; Amup Shah/Planet Earth Pictures 13, 24-25, 30, 32, 36-37, 55; A. & M. Shah/Planet Earth Pictures 46, 48-49, 148-149; Flip and Debra Shulke/Planet Earth Pictures 112; The Tiger Trust

Picture Library 105, 146, 150; Gunter Ziesler/Bruce Coleman Ltd 11, 16, 17, 22, 60-61; Jean-Pierre Zwaenepoel/Bruce Coleman Ltd 14, 21, 33, 34, 35, 53, 57, 84-85, 128-129.

Line illustration by E.H. Shepard copyright under the Berne Convention, reproduced by permission of Curtis Brown, London and Dutton, a division of Penguin USA, New York 95.

Every effort has been made to trace all copyright holders. The publishers wish to apologise for any errors or omissions.

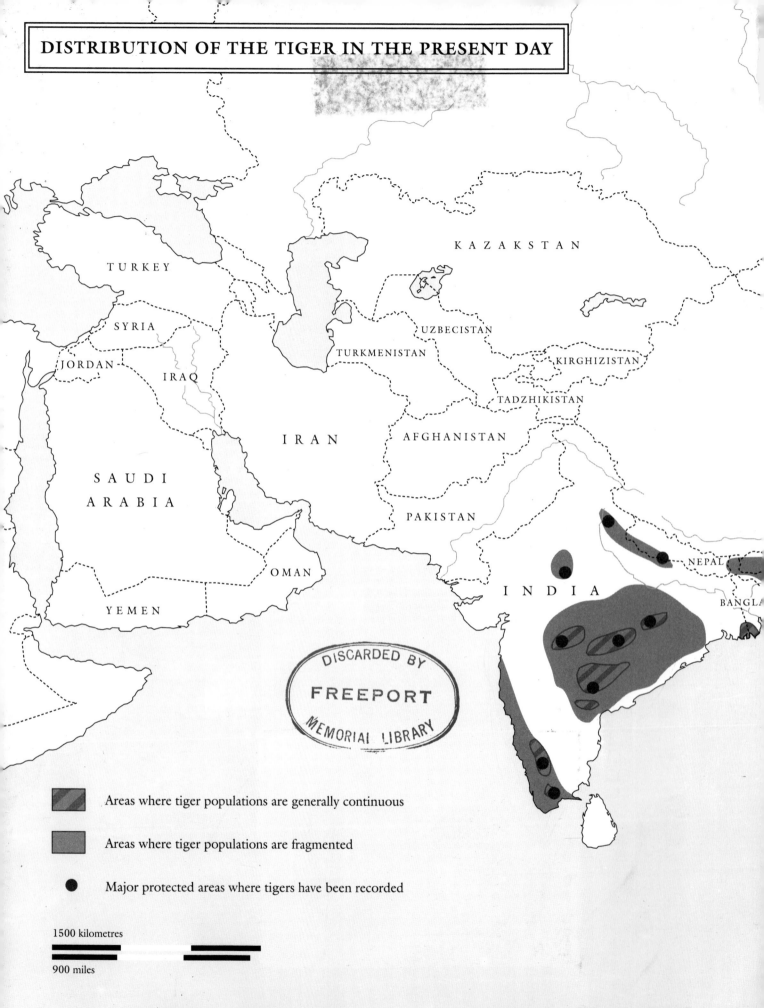

DISTRIBUTION OF THE TIGER IN THE PRESENT DAY

KAZAKSTAN

TURKEY

SYRIA

JORDAN

IRAQ

UZBECISTAN

TURKMENISTAN

KIRGHIZISTAN

TADZHIKISTAN

AFGHANISTAN

IRAN

PAKISTAN

SAUDI
ARABIA

OMAN

YEMEN

INDIA

NEPAL

BANGLA

Areas where tiger populations are generally continuous

Areas where tiger populations are fragmented

Major protected areas where tigers have been recorded

1500 kilometres

900 miles

(Peter Jackson, Chairman, IUCN Cat Specialist Group)